THE ULTIMATE UNOFFICIAL
ENCYCLOPEDIA
FOR
MINECRAFTERS
EARTH

AN A–Z GUIDE TO UNLOCKING INCREDIBLE ADVENTURES, BUILDPLATES, MOBS, RESOURCES, AND MOBILE GAMING FUN

MEGAN MILLER

Sky Pony Press
New York

Copyright © 2021 by Hollan Publishing, Inc.
Minecraft® is a registered trademark of Notch Development AB.
The Minecraft game is copyright © Mojang AB.

Sky Pony Press books may be purchased in bulk at special discounts for sales promotion,
corporate gifts, fund-raising, or educational purposes. Special editions can also be created
to specifications. For details, contact the Special Sales Department, Sky Pony Press, 307
West 36th Street, 11th Floor, New York, NY 10018 or info@skyhorsepublishing.com.

Sky Pony® is a registered trademark of Skyhorse Publishing, Inc.®, a Delaware corporation.

Visit our website at www.skyponypress.com.

10 9 8 7 6 5 4 3 2 1

Library of Congress Cataloging-in-Publication Data is available on file.

Cover design by Kai Texel
Cover art by Megan Miller

Print ISBN: 978-1-5107-6195-7
Ebook ISBN: 978-1-5107-6570-2

Printed in China

This work is based on the Early Access version of Minecraft Earth R20, and some aspects
of the game may have changed between writing this book and publication. For more
information on the most recent updates to Minecraft Earth, visit the Minecraft Help
Center at Help.minecraft.net.

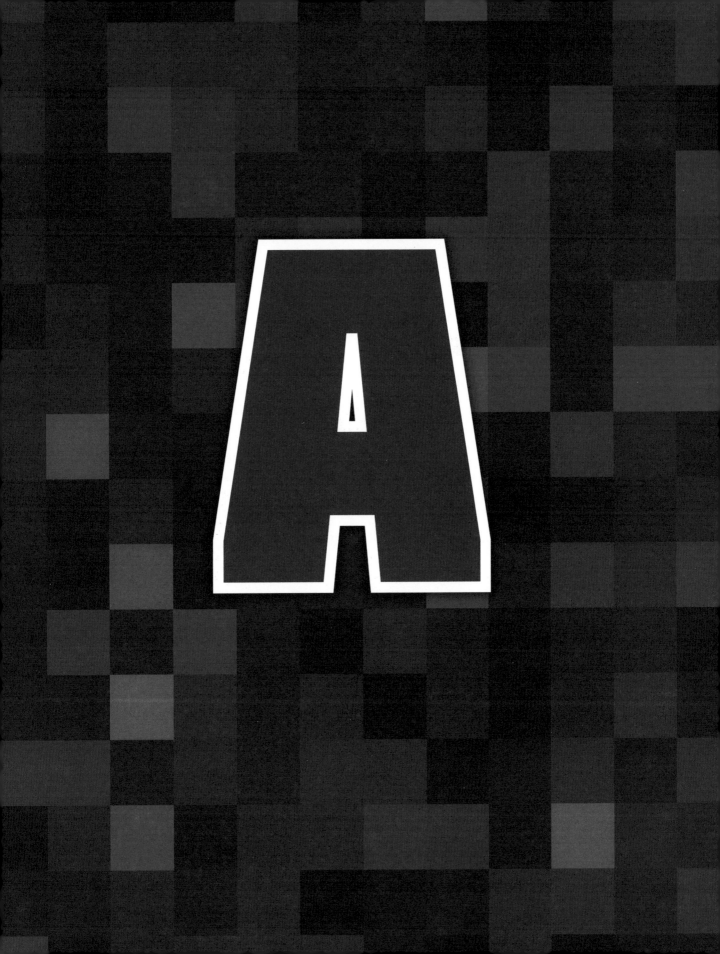

ACACIA LOGS

Acacia logs are a crafting resource and building block that you can get by chopping Acacia trees with an axe. You can craft them into planks or right-click them with an axe (you'll have to place them on a buildplate first) to remove their bark and create a "stripped" log version.

ACACIA SAPLINGS

Acacia saplings are what you need if you want to grow an acacia tree. Saplings are sometimes dropped when the leaves of the tree decay or are broken, and you can find them in Grass and Pond tappables. Plant them on dirt or grass, and use bone meal on them if you want to speed up the growing process.

ACACIA TREE

Acacia trees, with their gray bark and spreading, gray-green canopy, find their home in Minecraft's Dry Savannah biome. In Minecraft Earth, you can find acacia saplings in grass and pond tappables. Plant them on dirt, coarse dirt, or grass to have them grow into full-fledged trees, or use bone meal on them (you may need more than one) to grow them quickly. Chop them down for Acacia logs, and then you can craft them into orange acacia planks.

ACACIA WOOD PLANKS

Acacia planks are an orangey wood plank crafted from acacia logs. They can be used as a general wood resource in many recipes requiring wood, like sticks and beds and bowls. You can make stairs and slabs from acacia plank, as well as some wood-type specific items, like acacia wood buttons, doors, trapdoors, fences, and gates.

ACTIVATOR RAIL

Activator Rails are a type of rail used sometimes in minecart tracks. They are typically used singly, in between regular or powered rails. Their chief function is to emit a redstone signal when a minecart passes over them, which can then be used to power another redstone component or functional block, like a redstone lamp. They are crafted with 6 iron ingots, two sticks, and a redstone torch. You can find them in some Adventure chests.

ACTIVITY LOG

Your activity log is found in your Profile pages. It lists the tappables you've collected (and time!), in-game gifts you've received, challenges you've completed, and more, for every day you've played the game.

ADVENTURES

Adventures are the battle and looting grounds of Minecraft Earth. Classic outdoors Adventures are located outside in public areas like parks (this has been disabled during COVID-19 quarantines). Crystal Adventures are Adventures you can load in any location. An Adventure is similar to a buildplate, in that it is a digital "setting" that your mobile device can virtually place on a nearby surface. However, unlike buildplates, you do place these on ground surfaces as you play them at life size. An Adventure will appear at first as a small setting, like a pig sty or a few trees on a patch of grass. When you break these blocks with pickaxes and axes and shovels, you'll find a hidden location beneath; one that's possibly filled with skeletons now shooting at you. You must battle hostile mobs with your sword and collect materials with your pickaxe and axe. A few ores like iron, diamond, coal, gold, and lapis are typically hidden behind water flows and other blocks in small veins of 1 to 3 blocks. It can take a bit of searching and breaking to find them. You'll also want to locate and break the Adventure chest—it may be hidden behind other blocks, and if you find it, you'll get rare loot, including an Adventure crystal. If you're battling mobs, watch your health bar. Each strike against you damages you, and if your health bar depletes, you'll be dead and bounced out of the Adventure without any loot, any inventory, or any experience points. You can guard against this by using "boosts" in your play. There are different levels of Adventures: levels 1 to 3 for outdoors Adventures and common through epic for Crystal Adventures. The higher the level, the more hostile the mobs and the harder the Adventure is to complete.

Outdoor Adventures are displayed with a beacon on your World Map, and you must be within the blue radius to place and play them.

ADVENTURE CHESTS

Inside every Adventure is an Adventure chest of fairly rare loot. Although it's often hidden behind other blocks, the chests give off sparkly particles that give away their location. These chests have a few harder to get items which may include carrots, potatoes, rare blocks and ores, as well as weapons, tools, Adventure crystals, and mobs you can store in your inventory and later place on a buildplate. There are five levels of Adventure chests with increasing values of contained loot: common, uncommon, rare, epic, and legendary.

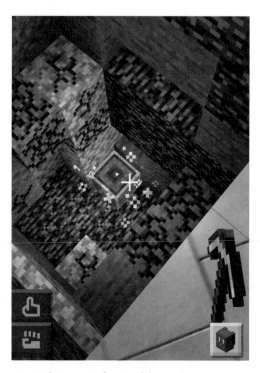

Adventure chests emit sparkles, so you can sometimes spot them when they are hidden behind other objects.

ADVENTURE CRYSTALS

Adventure crystals are an item you get from completing some challenges and from Adventure chests. Each Adventure crystal allows you to activate and play one Adventure, and the rarity or level of the crystal determines the rarity or level of the Adventure. For example, a common Adventure crystal will let you play a common Adventure. The levels are: common, uncommon, rare, epic, and legendary. The higher the level, the more difficult the Adventure. Crystals are stored on your Adventures page, and you can only store a maximum of three crystals for each level.

ADVENTURE XP BOOST

The Adventure XP Boost increases the amount of XP (experience points) you get from completing an Adventure. Level I lasts for 10 minutes and gives you 50% more XP; Level II lasts 15 minutes and gives 75% more XP; and Level III lasts 30 minutes and doubles your XP. You can also purchase a toy mini-figure called "Slowed Creeper" that, when activated (scanned into your mobile device), will give you a Level I strength Adventure XP Boost.

ALBINO COW

You can find this white-furred, red-eyed bovine variant in Cow tappables. Despite its unusual looks, it is pretty much a regular cow. [Health: 10]

AMBER CHICKEN

The Amber Chicken is a passive chicken mob that's new to Minecraft Earth. It's exactly like a regular chicken, but sports feathers with the reddish golden color of amber. (Amber is the fossilized resin of ancient trees that is treated like a gem and used in jewelry and decoration.) You can find amber chickens in Chicken tappables. [Health: 4]

ANDESITE

Andesite is a type of stone and in Minecraft Earth it is found below ground where other stone blocks are found. It has a rough, variegated gray surface. You can find it regularly in Adventures and in some buildplates as well as collect it from Stone tappables. You can craft it into andesite stairs and slabs, polished andesite blocks, and polished andesite stairs and slabs. You can also craft it by combining a diorite block with a cobblestone block.

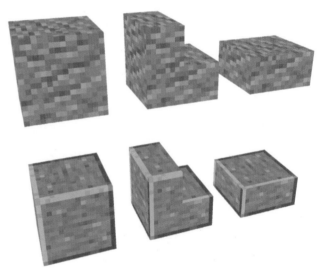

APPLES

Apples are a fruit that in Minecraft come from oak trees—specifically, the oak tree leaf blocks. Each oak leaf block, when it is broken or when it decays, has a small chance of generating an apple which will fall to the ground. In Minecraft Earth, you can also find them in some Adventure chests.

ARROW

You'll need arrows to shoot a bow, and to craft them you need sticks, flint, and feathers. They're also a possible drop from any skeletons you kill.

ASHEN COW

Another cow variant, the Ashen cow is similar to a regular cow but fully gray-furred with a darker gray stripe down its back. You can find it in Cow tappables. [Health: 10]

ATTACK BOOST

If you want to spend some rubies, you can purchase an Attack Boost in the Store to increase the amount of damage you deal when striking mobs in an Adventure. A Level I Attack Boost lasts 10 minutes and gives you 25% more attack damage; Level II gives you 50% more attack damage for 15 minutes; and Level III gives you 100% more attack damage for 30 minutes. You can also purchase toy mini-figures that will give you a Level I strength Attack Boost, "Attacking Alex," "Attacking Steve," and "Poisoning Enderman."

AUGMENTED REALITY (AR)

Augmented reality (AR) refers to the use of digital data to overlay on real-world imagery (often on a mobile device). As an AR game, Minecraft Earth displays game elements, like Adventures and buildplates, on live visual photographic images from a mobile device. It places tappables on a map that is based on real-World Maps.

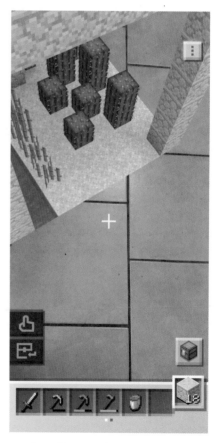

In augmented reality applications, digital images, like this buildplate, are overlaid or combined with real world data, like the images from a mobile device.

AXE

If you want to chop down trees quickly for their logs, or other wood-based blocks, like fences and planks, you'll need an axe. Axes can be made of (in order of material strength) wood planks, stone, gold, iron, and diamond and are more durable and faster the higher the level of material. To craft an axe you'll need a stick and your chosen material—3 of each. and you may also find an axe in Adventure chests. You also use an axe to right-click a log to strip it of its bark.

AZURE BLUETS

Azure bluets are one of Minecraft X's small flowers (fitting into a 1 block space). It is found in Plains and Flower Forest biomes and can be crafted into light gray dye. You can find Azure bluets in Grass and Pond tappables as well as many Adventures and buildplates.

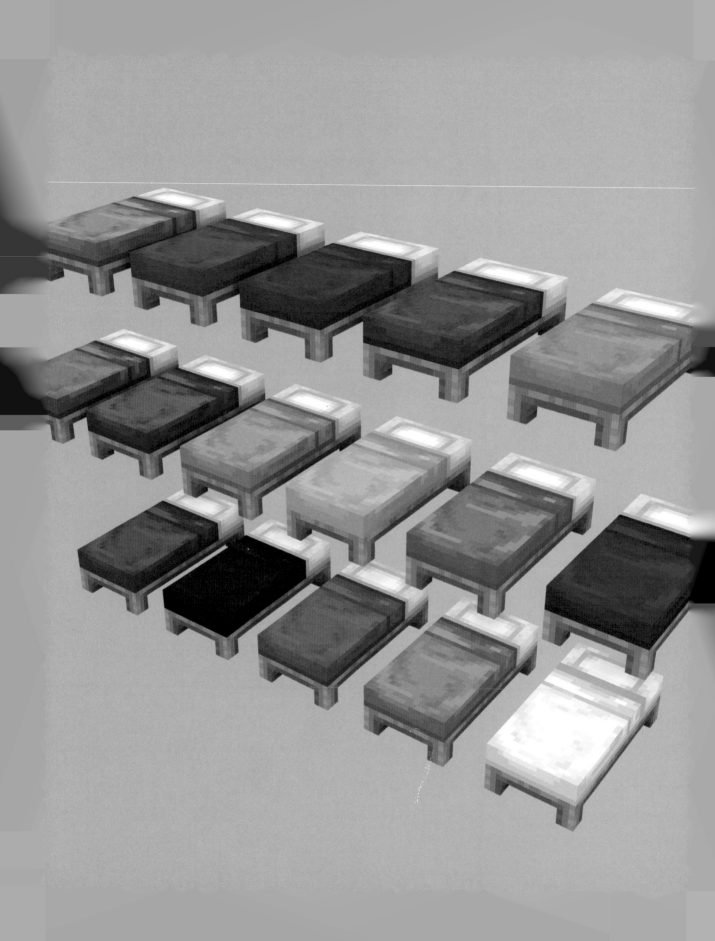

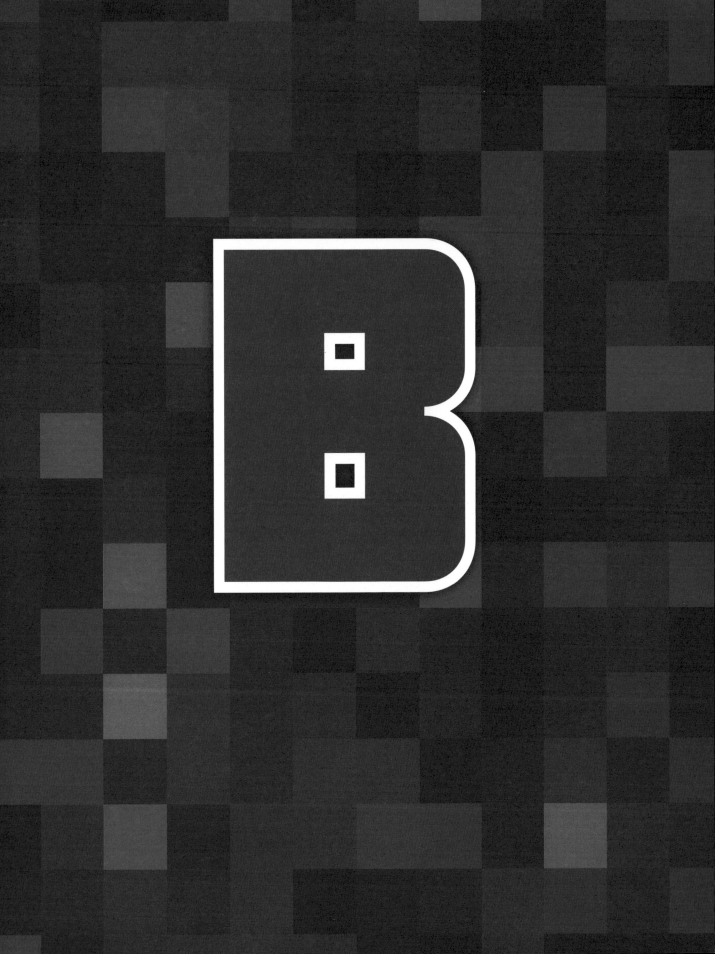

BACKPACK

The backpack is a temporary inventory space that opens up, empty, when you start an Adventure. It will automatically hold any goodies you get that don't fit into your hotbar. When your Adventure is over, the backpack's contents are transferred to your main inventory—unless you die, of course. If you die in an Adventure, your hotbar and backpack contents are lost. You can, however, use Keeper and Hoarding boosts (purchasable with rubies) to prevent this.

In an Adventure, your backpack button is above your hotbar on the right.

BAKED POTATO

Baked potatoes are a good food source. You'll need to grow potatoes on a buildplate and then cook them in a furnace, although you might find them in a common Adventure chest. They'll replenish 4 health points when you eat them.

BEDS

Beds are a decorative item in Minecraft Earth. They're crafted from wool blocks (which may be dyed to give the bed a colored bedspread) and wood planks. You can find beds on some Adventures and buildplates.

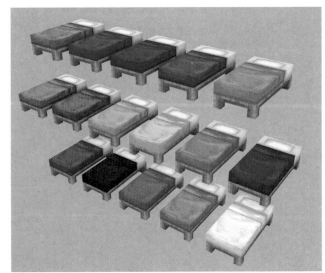

BEDROCK

Bedrock is a black and gray block in Minecraft that cannot be broken or destroyed. It is used to border and end the Minecraft game or play areas, so you'll find it bordering the underground scenes in Adventures and at the very bottom of buildplates.

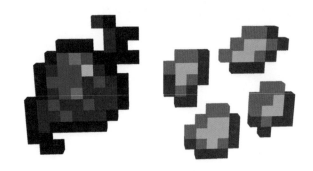

BEETROOT SOUP

You can craft a nourishing bowl of Beetroot Soup with six beets and wooden bowl; eating it will restore 6 health points (HP). You can find beetroot soup in some Adventure chests.

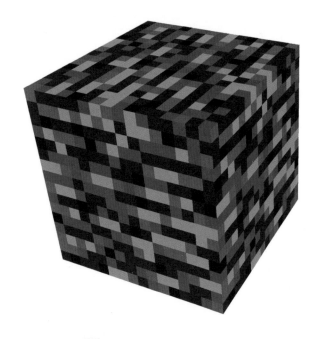

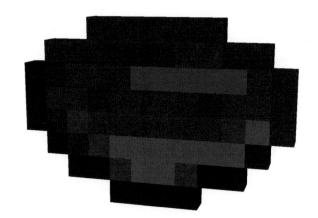

BEETROOT

Beetroots are a crop vegetable in Minecraft, meaning you can plant them on farmland, grow them, and eat them to restore 2 HP. To plant them, you'll need beetroot seeds and watered farmland. You can get beetroot and beetroot seeds from common Adventure chests and beetroot seeds from Chest tappables.

BIOMES

Biomes are the different environments in nature that support different plants and animals. In Minecraft, biomes may have different grass and sky colors, different precipitation (rain or snow), as well as different mobs, trees, flowers, and terrain. Each buildplate is set in a specific biome, which may be Desert, Jungle, Plains, Snowy Tundra, Forest, and the Dark Forest (with dark oaks and giant mushrooms). Other Minecraft biomes include Birch Forest, Savanna (with acacia trees), Swamp, and Taiga.

This buildplate is set in the Jungle biome, which is home to jungle trees, parrots, ocelots, and more.

BIRCH LEAVES

Birch leaves are blocks that make up the canopy of the Birch tree, and behave much like other leaf blocks—they can be collected by using shears, broken with your hand or other tools. If you break them or the leaves decay, they have a chance of dropping a stick or a sapling. Unlike most other leaves, birch leaves stay the same color in any biome they are placed in.

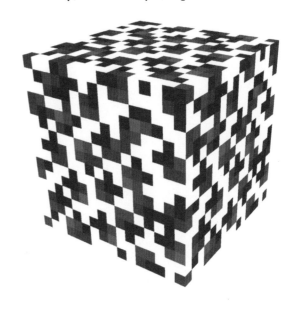

BIRCH LOGS

Birch logs are the blocks that make up the trunks of Birch trees. They have a white bark, mottled with horizontal black markings. You can craft them into birch planks or use an axe to turn them into stripped birch logs. You can find them in Birch tappables and in some Adventures and buildplates.

BIRCH SAPLINGS

Birch saplings can be planted to grow birch trees, and you can use bone meal on them to make them grow faster. You can get birch saplings from decaying birch leaves and from Birch tappables.

BIRCH TREE

Birch trees have white bark mottled with dark patches. You can chop them with an axe for white and black birch logs and craft the logs into the pale beige wood planks. You'll find their saplings in Birch tappables.

BIRCH TAPPABLE

Birch tappables are one of the three types of tree tappable, along with Oak tappables and Spruce tappables. You can collect birch saplings and birch logs from them.

BIRCH WOOD PLANKS

Birch planks have a pale beige color and are often used decoratively in modern-styled buildings in Minecraft. You can use them as fuel, in recipes that require any wood. Birch planks are also used to craft birch buttons, doors, trapdoors, fences, and gates. You can find birch planks in some Adventures and buildplates.

BLOCKS

Minecraft is a game whose world is based on "blocks," 1x1x1 meter cubes of material that you can break and replace and combine to construct whatever you please. Trees are made of blocks (log blocks and leaf blocks), and the ground is made of blocks (grass blocks, dirt blocks, stone blocks), and even things that aren't cubically shaped take up the space of a single block, like fences, flowers, doors, and glass panes. Blocks can be placed in the world and on top of one another. Except for a very few gravity-affected blocks, once you've placed a block it will stay there, even if you remove the block beneath it. Gravity-affected blocks include sand, gravel, anvils, and concrete powder. For gravity-affected blocks, if you remove the block they are placed on, they'll fall to stand on the next block below. (In some cases, the falling block will revert into their item form, if the block below is what is called a "non-solid" like a torch.)

BLUE ORCHIDS

Blue orchids are a flower found traditionally only in the Swamp biome in Minecraft. In Minecraft Earth, you can find them in Grass and Pond tappables and in some buildplates.

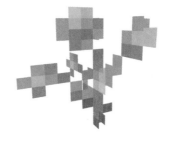

BONES

Bones are a material you can use for crafting bone meal, and you can get them from killing skeletons, as well as fish, bone spiders, and skeleton wolves. You can also find them in common Adventure chests. You can also find bone blocks as building materials in some Adventures and in some Adventure chests. Bones can be crafted into 3 bone meal, and bone blocks can be crafted into 9 bone meal. You can also craft 9 bone meal into bone blocks.

BONE BLOCKS

Bone blocks are used in Minecraft to create large fossils of unknown creatures. A bone block can be crafted into (or from) 9 bone meal. You can find bone blocks in some Adventure chests and Adventures.

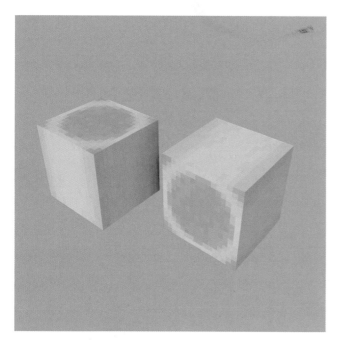

BONE MEAL

It doesn't sound very tasty but you don't have to eat it. Bone meal is a very helpful item in Minecraft that you use it as fertilizer to make some plants grow faster. To use it, just right-click the plant with bone meal in your hand; it may take one, several, or many uses of bone meal to grow the plant fully. Plants that will grow with bone meal include crop plants, bamboo, saplings, flowers, grass, ferns, mushrooms, and cocoa beans. Cactus is an exception; you can't use bone meal to make it grow.

You can also use bone meal right on a grass block to create some random tall grass, grass, and flowers on it and on grass blocks surrounding it.

In addition, you can craft bone meal into white dye, which you can use to dye some objects like wool, and combine with other dyes to create new dyes.

You can get bone meal by crafting bones or bone blocks and killing bone spiders. You can also find it in Chest tappables and in some Adventure chests.

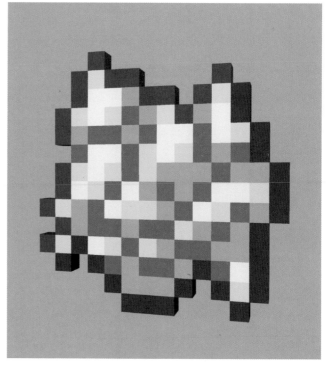

BONE SPIDER

Can a spider get any scarier? This Minecraft Earth–only spider is actually an extra-strong hybrid of spider and skeleton, and in addition to regular spider attack damage it can also shoot you with bones shard in a dangerous ranged attack. Kill it and it may drop string, bones, and/or bone meal. You can find it in Adventures and sometimes in Adventure chests and in the Level 25 buildplate. [Health: 32]

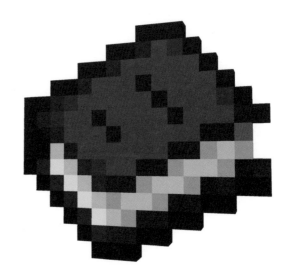

BOOKSHELVES

Bookshelves are a decorative block in Minecraft that you can craft or find in Adventure chests, and some Adventures and buildplates.

BOOKS

You can craft books in Minecraft from paper (from sugarcane) and leather (from cows). Books are used to craft bookshelves, a decorative block.

BOOSTS

Boosts are perks to gameplay that you can either purchase with rubies or purchase through real-life toy action figures at department stores. Boosts change some game functions to your advantage for a short period of time, speeding up crafting time or giving you more attack damage for an Adventure. You can only use boosts from an action figure once a day.

In-game boosts can be purchased through the Minecraft Earth store and they come with three levels. Higher levels increase the duration and power of the boost.

BOOST MINIS

Boost minis are Minecraft mini-figures with boosts produced by the toy company Mattel. You can find them in video game and department stores. Each figure will give you a special boost or power, similar to the in-game boosts, that lasts for 10 minutes and can only be used once every 24 hours.

Click Boosts in the side menu and then the mini-figure icon to open up the Boost Mini page, where you'll see which you've purchased and which are active. Here, Enraged Golem and Undying Evoker are available but not currently active.

BOW

Bows are the primary Minecraft ranged weapon—they allow you to damage an opponent from a distance. (In Minecraft Earth, however, swords also act as a ranged weapon, and you can hit foes in dungeons below without a problem.) Each use of the bow will remove one arrow from your inventory. You'll need arrows in your hotbar to use bows, and a stick and three strings to craft them. You can also find them as loot from various Adventure chests.

BOWL

Bowls are one of the few items in Minecraft that are only a crafting resource; you don't use them by themselves for anything. You craft them from three planks and use them to make soups and stews.

BREAD

Bread is craftable from 4 wheat and eatable, restoring 6 health points, making it an excellent food source in Minecraft Earth. You can also find bread in some Adventure chests.

BRICKS

The classic, red-brick block is a common building block in Minecraft, and you craft it from 4 single bricks (brick items). Single bricks you create by smelting clay balls. Brick blocks can also be crafted into brick slabs and brick stairs. You can find brick blocks in some Adventure chests, Adventures, and buildplates, and you can also find separate brick items from Adventure chests.

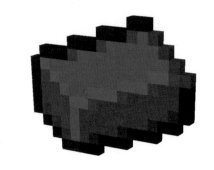

BUCKET

Buckets are a functional item in Minecraft: you use them for picking up and placing water, mud, and lava. You can also milk cows with buckets, and pick up fish with them. You craft them with three iron ingots, but you can also find buckets in Chest tappables as well as Adventure chests.

BUILDPLATES

Buildplates are square platforms in Minecraft Earth where you can create your own settings and creations by placing blocks and entities on them. They come prebuilt, and you can customize these scenes, or harvest them for blocks and resources and start your own build. Buildplates range in size from 8 x 8 blocks to 32 x 32 blocks and some come with some rare mobs, like the Mob of Me and mooblooms.

There are both free and buyable buildplates in the game. Free buildplates are locked until you reach specific levels of experience points. Other buildplates are purchasable with rubies.

Buildplates are all square and range in size from 8x8 blocks (width and length) to 32x32 blocks. Buildplates include several below ground levels, the lowest of which is made from bedrock. They can be built up to 221 blocks high. Buildplates also come as either Nighttime or Daytime scenes, and with a specific biome, such as Plains or Icy Tundra.

To play with a buildplate, you must "place" it on a real-world flat surface as seen through your mobile device's camera. You can choose to place it in Build mode or Play mode. In Build mode, the buildplate is displayed at a small size so that you can more easily see all of the build and modify it. In Play mode, the buildplate is shown at real-life size, with blocks taking up a 1 meter cubed space. In Play mode, any changes you make to the build aren't saved.

You can invite nearby friends to play or build on a buildplate with you, or you can share a link of your buildplate with a friend. These shared buildplates are also in a temporary "Play mode" instance, and so changes made to the buildplates won't last beyond the play session or affect your buildplate.

The entries for buildplates in the store and buildplates area will tell you a buildplate's size and what special mobs are on it; you can click the information button [i] for a description and list of featured items.

BUTTERCUPS

Buttercups are a Minecraft Earth unique flower. They are spread by the moobloom when it meanders around on grass. You can get them from using shears on a moobloom, or find them in Grass and Pond tappables as well as some Adventures and buildplates.

You can find out more about items, mobs, and blocks in the Journal; just tap the items icon to open up a page of details. Here, you find out what biome the buttercup is associated with, its rarity, and what tools you can harvest it with.

BUTTONS

Buttons are a redstone power source in Minecraft. When you place them on a block and press them, they emit a short redstone pulse, in a way that's similar to electricity. This pulse will cause other adjacent blocks that interact to redstone pulses to react. For example, a button next to a door can open and shut that door. Button can be made from stone and all types of wood planks. You can find them in some Adventures.

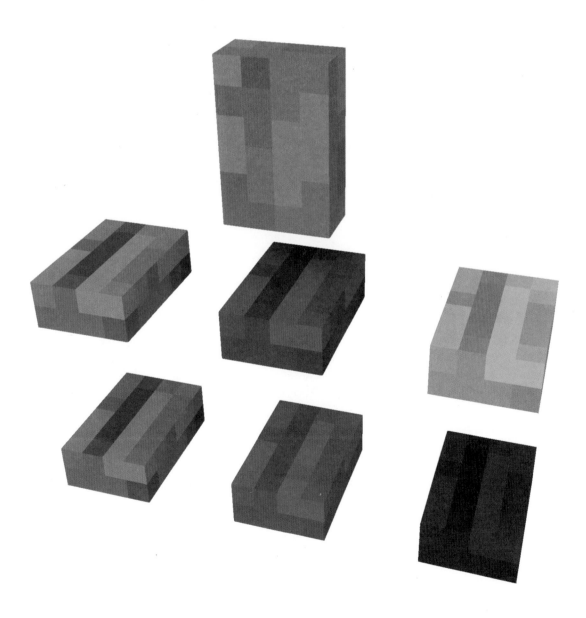

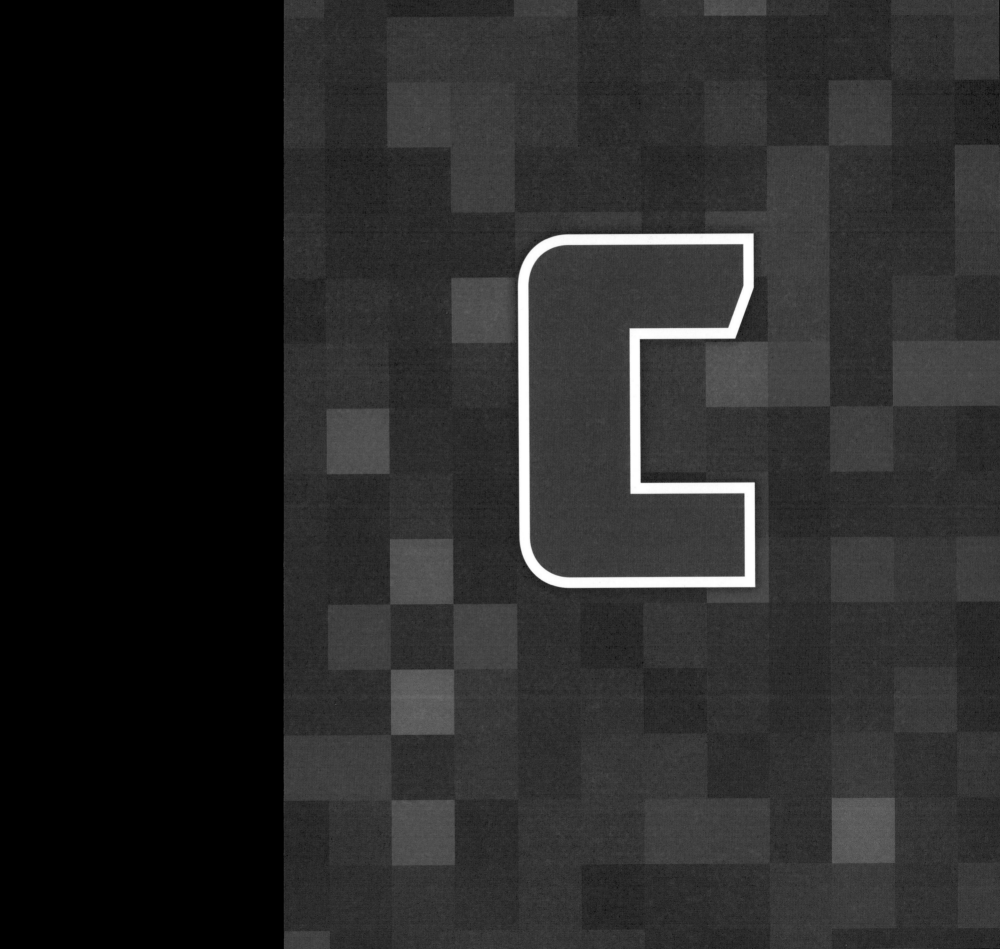

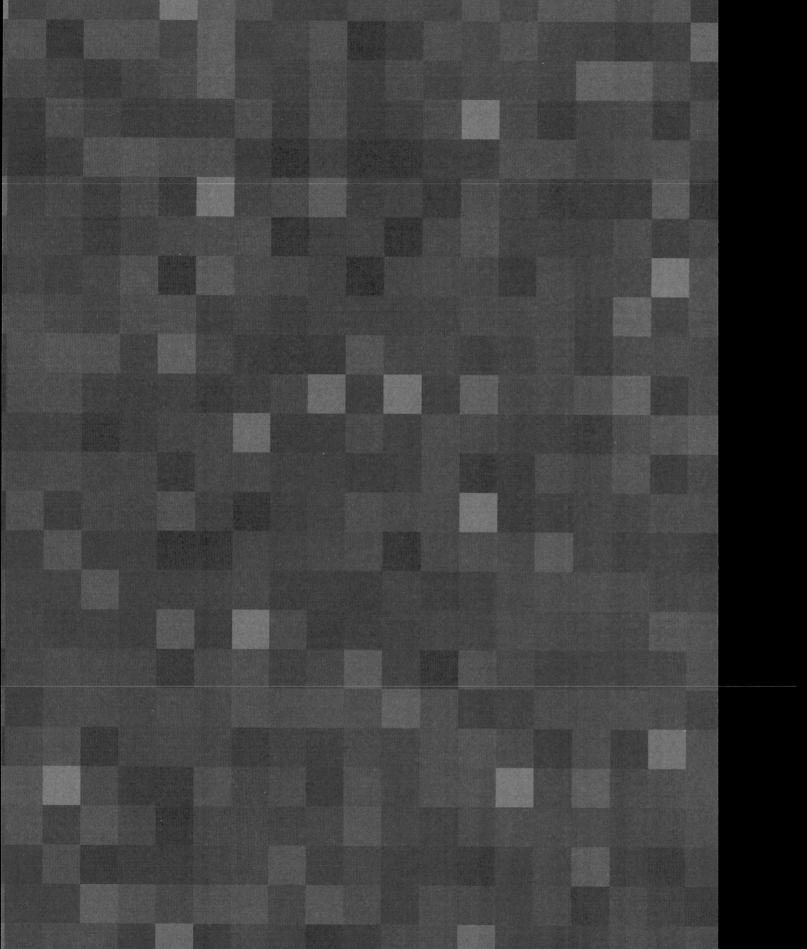

CACTUS

Cactus is a plant in Minecraft's Desert biomes, and you can grow it only on sand, and it doesn't need any water nearby. It must be free-standing—you can't place a cactus block alongside any other block, and it only grows three blocks high. Its spikes will damage any mobs that touch it, and items that fall on it will be destroyed. To harvest cactus, simply break the first, second, or third block, or the sand it is growing on. Any cactus blocks above the block you break will also drop. The cactus blocks can be smelted into green dye. You can find cactus in some Adventures and buildplates.

CAREER CHALLENGES

Career challenges are one of the three types of general challenges you can access through the trophy icon on the sidebar. These will guide you through the main gameplay areas, like collecting, crafting, and building. Career challenges are progressive, so you must finish one stage or set of challenges to unlock the next.

CARPET

Carpet is a decorative, thin block that you place on other blocks. You craft it using white or dyed wool blocks. Carpet is found in some Adventures and buildplates.

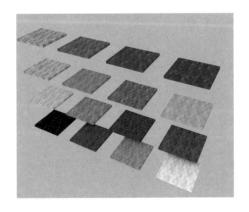

CARROT

The carrot is a food and a crop plant in Minecraft, meaning that you can grow it on farmland. You use an entire carrot as your planting seed, and it will go through several stages until the top leaves are full and the tops of the carrots showing are bright orange. You can use bone meal on carrots to make them grow faster. When you harvest the grown carrot plant, you'll usually get several carrots back for your effort. Eating a carrot will restore just 1 health point. You can get carrots from Adventure chests and as a rare drop from a zombie.

CAULDRON

A cauldron is a large black pot that can hold one block of water. You can craft it from iron ingots, or get it from Adventure chests, Adventures, or buildplates.

CHALLENGES

Challenges are gameplay tasks that you can perform to gain more experience and sometimes special loot. There are three types of general challenges: Daily, which renew every day; Tappables, which involve gathering resources and placing things on buildplates; and Career, which guide you through gameplay. These challenges are found through the Trophy icon on the sidebar. In addition, there are Seasonal challenges, which last about 2 weeks, and you can find these through the Globe icon in the sidebar.

CHARACTER CREATOR

The Character Creator is where you go to change your avatar's appearance, sometimes called your "skin." This includes your height, shape, and costume. Initially in the game, there are two premade skins for you to choose from: the classic "Steve" and "Alex" skins from the original Java edition of Minecraft. To change your skin, open the Characters area in your Profile, and then click Edit to open the Dressing Room. Here you can choose from free or buyable skins or skin elements like hats and shoes.

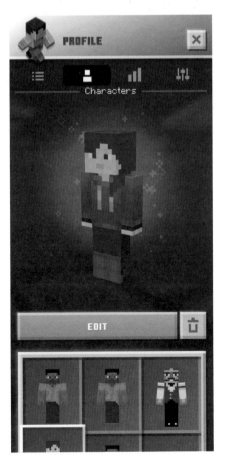

CHARCOAL

Charcoal is a fuel in Minecraft that you use to smelt items with in a furnace. It looks very similar to coal but is slightly grayer. You can make charcoal by smelting wood logs. You can also use charcoal to craft torches.

CHEST TAPPABLE

Chest tappables appear on the World Map and tapping them will get you 1–3 game items or objects. These can include beetroot seeds, bone meal, brown dye, buckets, bucket of mud, clay, clay blocks, cobblestone walls, cobweb, cocoa beans, common Adventure crystals, flowerpot, glass blocks, glowstone dust, gunpowder, ink sacs, iron bars, levers, minecarts, Mobs of Me,

nether quartz, note block, oak planks (blocks, slabs, or stairs) oak doors, oak fences, oak gates, oak pressure plate, polished andesite (blocks, slabs, or stairs), polished diorite (blocks, slabs, or stairs), polished granite (blocks, slabs, or stairs), powered rails, rails, redstone lamps, redstone repeaters, redstone torches, stone brick blocks, TNT, and torches.

CHICKEN

The chicken is an iconic Minecraft passive mob, and it and many variants have been brought into Minecraft Earth. Unlike most mobs, which can fall and take fall damage, chickens can slowly flutter down. Minecraft Earth chicken variants include the Amber Chicken, the Midnight Chicken, the Stormy Chicken, and the Cluckshroom. When you kill them, they will drop raw chickens, feathers, and sometimes eggs. You can find them in Chicken tappables and some buildplates and Adventures. [Health: 4]

CHICKEN TAPPABLE

Chicken tappables are one of the four mob tappables, including sheep, cows, and pigs. Loot you can get from them includes feathers, eggs, and chickens or a chicken variant, like Amber, Midnight, and Stormy chickens and cluckshrooms.

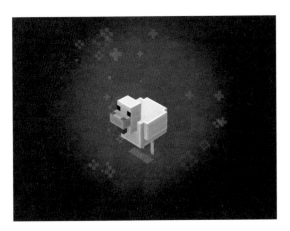

CLAY

Clay is a Minecraft resource material that comes in either a ball shape or block. It is found as clay blocks in the banks and beds of rivers, lakes, and oceans, and the block drops four clay balls when you break it. You can recraft the clay balls back into clay blocks. Additionally, you can smelt clay balls into bricks and clay balls into blocks of terracotta. You can find clay in Chest and Pond tappables and clay blocks in common Adventure chests.

CLUCKSHROOM

The cluckshroom is a Minecraft Earth hybrid mob: a cross between a chicken and a red mushroom. It looks and acts a bit like a chicken, but it prefers to stay in dark (protected from the sky) areas, where it will spawn mushrooms as it pecks about. The cluckshroom also drops raw chicken and feathers when killed, and you can

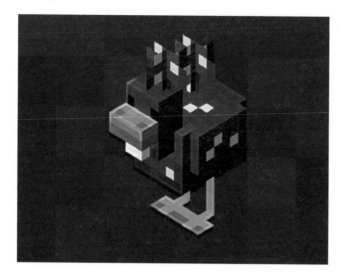

find it in Chicken tappables, as well as some buildplates and Adventures. [Health: 4]

COAL

Coal is a common fuel material in Minecraft that you get from mining coal ore in Adventures. Coal is also used to craft torches, and you can craft it into coal blocks, which can be re-crafted into 9 coal. You can get coal blocks from Adventure chests and get coal as loot from killing Furnace Golems.

COAL ORE

Coal ore is found in small veins (often 1-2 ore blocks) in Adventures and in the Hearth Home buildplate. Mining them with a pick (even a wooden pick works) will drop the coal item, which you can use as fuel.

COARSE DIRT

Coarse dirt is a dirt variant that you can craft from two dirt and two gravel. It has a slightly darker, more mottled appearance than dirt. Unlike dirt, nearby grass blocks won't convert it to grass, so it is useful in builds where you want dirt blocks placed next to grass. Like dirt, you can plant flowers and other plants

COCOA BEANS

Cocoa beans are a seed you can plant on the side of a jungle oak log. When they grow from a pale greenish color to a warm brown, you can harvest them and use them as an ingredient in cookies or craft them into brown dye.

on it. You can find coarse dirt in Grass and Pond tappables as well as Adventures and buildplates.

COBBLESTONE

Cobblestone is an iconic Minecraft building block that is produced when you mine stone with a pickaxe. It is a primary building and resource block and can be crafted into slabs, stairs, and walls, and smelted into stone. There is also a rarer mossy cobblestone variant that can be crafted from cobblestone and vines. Cobblestone can be created naturally when flowing lava (not a lava source block) touches the side of a water block, and the flowing lava becomes cobblestone. (Two other water/lava interactions produce stone and obsidian).

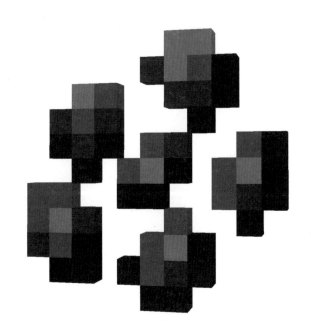

COBWEB

Cobwebs are decorative blocks used in many builds. They will slow down a mob or player that passes through it or brushes up against it. They will even slow down falling entities. Getting trapped in a cobweb can be deadly if you're in the middle of a battle. You can use shears on a cobweb to get the cobweb block, otherwise, it will drop string if you break it with a sword.

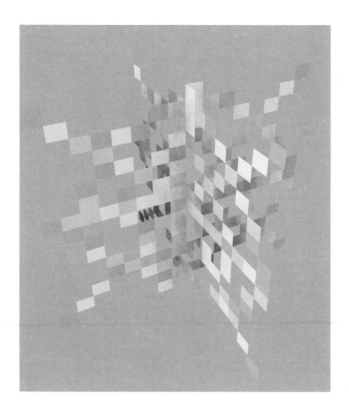

COD

Cod, also sometimes referred to in the game as fish, is a fish that can be dropped as raw cod from polar bears and some Adventures. You'll want to cook it for a nourishing meal.

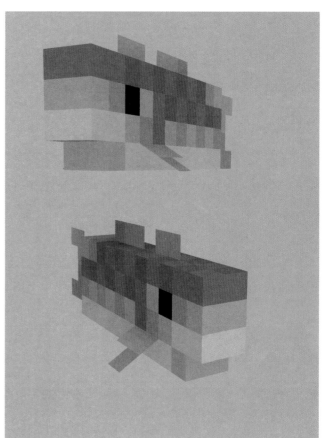

COMBAT

You'll encounter combat situations in Minecraft Earth when you embark on Adventures. Most Adventures (except in the lowest level) involve battling hostile mobs like skeletons, zombies, and creepers. Although you can use a bow, a sword is much handier. It can kill mobs at a distance and doesn't require arrows or loading times, and you'll want the strongest sword you can afford; iron or diamond, preferably. Some essential tactics in combat include food, as eating food regenerates health, block placement, and withdrawing. You can place blocks between yourself and hostile, below-ground areas (or only break narrow openings to them) as a shield to make it difficult for skeletons to shoot you and easy for you to get out of range. If your health is reaching low levels, you can step away from the Adventure buildplate's edges to avoid being visible or reachable by a mob in order to eat and regain health. Of course, this doesn't help if the mobs can reach ground level, but you can avoid this by making sure there are no steps or single-blocks in the build for them to climb on. Place blocks in the build to ensure there are rises of two blocks rather than one. (Spiders can still climb these walls, so be forewarned.)

COMPASS

The compass is an icon that displays at the top right of the World Map. When you start playing, The World Map has North at the top, and the compass needle points straight up. Your avatar in the middle of the World Map shows

you which direction you yourself (meaning your mobile device) are facing in real life (IRL). However, you can swipe in a circular motion on the World Map or change the phone's positioning to change the map's direction. As the map turns, the compass needle also swings to show you where North is. You can reset the compass and map to the same direction you are facing by clicking the compass icon, which will then show a "link" icon.

CONCRETE

Concrete is a building block that you make by placing concrete powder next to or in water. You can also pour water over concrete powder to make concrete. This block, known for its flat texture and bright appearance, comes in all 16 of the main Minecraft colors; the color comes from the dye used to create concrete powder.

COOKED BEEF

Cooked Beef is what you will get when you place raw beef (a drop from a killed cow) into a furnace in the Smelting area. It will restore 6 health points to your Health bar. You can also get cooked beef from some Adventure chests.

CONCRETE POWDER

Concrete powder is a building block that you craft from gravel, sand, and a dye to color it. You can use any of the sixteen Minecraft colored dyes to make it. If a concrete powder block is exposed to water, it will turn into a concrete block.

COOKED CHICKEN

Put the raw chicken drop from killing a chicken into a smelter and you will get a cooked chicken—a food that will replenish 4 health points when you eat it. You can also get cooked chicken in some Adventure chests.

COOKED MUTTON

Mutton is another word for lamb, and raw mutton is a drop from sheep when you kill them. As with any raw meat dropped from a farm animal, you can eat it as is, but it won't restore more than 1 health point. Now, if you cook that mutton to make cooked mutton, eating it will restore a full 6 health points. You might also find already cooked mutton in an Adventure chest.

COOKED COD

If you get some raw cod from an Adventure chest or by killing a polar bear (by accident of course), be sure to cook it up in a furnace, as this food will replenish 4 hunger points for you. You may also get some cooked cod from an Adventure chest.

COOKED PORKCHOP

If you guessed that a cooked porkchop comes from cooking a raw porkchop in a furnace, you are ahead of the game. A cooked porkchop will get you 7 of your valuable health points back. The sad part is that you have to kill a pig to get a porkchop, unless you find a porkchop in an Adventure chest.

COOKED RABBIT

Kill rabbit, get raw rabbit, cook rabbit, eat rabbit, get 4 health points back! You can find cooked rabbit in some Adventure chests.

COOKED SALMON

You will need raw salmon (which you can get from polar bears, live salmon, and some Adventure chests) in order to prepare a delicious cooked salmon. When you eat this delicious salmon, it will restore 4 health points on your health bar.

COOKIES

You can make eight cookies by crafting cocoa beans and 2 wheat together, and if you eat one it will restore 4 health points. You can find cookies in some Adventure chests.

CORNFLOWERS

Cornflowers are a small blue flower native to Minecraft's Plains and Flower Forest biomes. They're used to make blue dye, and you can find them in Adventures and buildplates.

COW

The cow is a beloved Minecraft farm animal that's been used as the basis for a number of variants and hybrids, including Albino cows, Ashen cows, Sunset cows, Wooly cows, and mooblooms. If you click a cow with a bucket in your hand, you'll get a bucket of milk. If you kill it, it can drop raw beef and leather. You can find cows in Cow tappables, as well as some Adventures and buildplates. [Health: 10]

COW TAPPABLE

The Cow tappable on the World Map is the main way to get a cow of any type, outside of a buildplate. You'll commonly get a regular cow, and the rarest cow variant you can get from a Cow tappable is the hybrid moobloom.

CRAFTERS GUIDE TO MINECRAFT EARTH

This website, at Craftersguide.stents.dev, is run by gamers who take an in-depth look at the code files of the Minecraft Earth game application. You can find details about almost all game elements, items, blocks, and mobs, as well as buildplates and Adventures. You can even view Adventures layer-by-layer to see where ores are placed.

CRAFTING

You can get some game resources from tappables and others from mining and looting during Adventures, but there are some blocks that can only be made (or gotten easily) by crafting. Crafting is the process of combining one or more items in a virtual crafting table or workbench that you can access by clicking the Make Stuff icon on the bottom menu. Here, you can access and select crafting recipes, and if you have the correct resources on hand, the game will take a little (or a lot) of time to then create the desired goods.

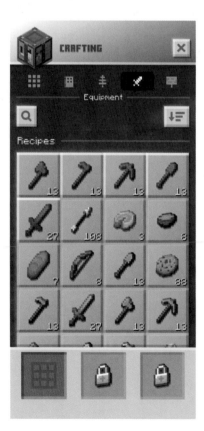

CRAFTING BOOST

The Crafting Boost makes crafting faster, for a period of time, for a cost of rubies. Level I increases the speed of crafting by 100% for 10 minutes. Level II triples the speed for 15 minutes, and Level III increases crafting speed by 700% for 30 minutes. You can also use the Mattel Minecraft Earth mini-figures "Crafting Steve" and "Crafting Alex" to give you a Level I strength crafting boost.

CREEPER

The creeper is arguably Minecraft's unique poster child and the source of many memes, with its distinguished mottled green and white skin and sorrowful frown. It is also known for the hiss it makes as it nears you and gets ready to explode. You'll want to kill this mob from a distance and not let it get closer than three blocks away. If it does, try to move away before it ignites. If you kill it, it can drop gunpowder. You can find creepers as loot from the rarer Adventure chests, rarely in Grass tappables, and encounter them in Adventures. [Health: 20]

CROPS

Plants you can grow for food or recipe ingredients in Minecraft include beetroot, carrots, sugarcane, cocoa beans, mushrooms, pumpkins, melons, potatoes, and wheat. All of these except for sugarcane, cocoa beans, and mushrooms require farmland to grow on.

CRYSTAL ADVENTURES

Crystal Adventures are pretty much identical to the original outdoor Adventures (which were removed during COVID-19 quarantines) except you can play at your home or wherever you are. You do need an Adventure crystal to play them. You can get common Adventure crystals from Chest tappables, and you also get crystals from completing some challenges. Adventure chests can also include Adventure crystals. There are currently four types of crystals, representing four difficulty levels of Adventures: common (Gray), uncommon (Green), rare (Blue), and epic (Purple).

Each Crystal Adventure has an Adventure chest, which may be hidden, or appear only after you've achieved a goal such as solving a puzzle. The overall goal of Adventures is to defeat the mobs, solve any puzzles (not all Adventures have puzzles), mine and gather ores and other resources, and find the Adventure chest for its goodies. Ores are often hidden behind other blocks, water, or lava, and there are often only a handful of ore blocks in an Adventure.

You only have a set amount of time (about 10 minutes) to complete an Adventure, but an hourglass timer appears to show you when time is nearly up.

You can only take whatever is in your hotbar into an Adventure—you'll have no access

to your inventory. As you gather materials that need storage beyond your hotbar, they will be stored in a temporary inventory called the backpack. You can access this backpack while you're in the Adventure. However, when the Adventure is over, anything in your backpack will be sent to your main inventory. If you die during an Adventure, you'll lose your entire hotbar inventory, swords and all, as well as any experience or other resources you've gathered. You can use boosts to prevent losing your inventory.

"CURSED" BLOCKS

A few, harder-difficulty Adventures have certain blocks that you must remove in order to stop enemies from spawning. These are sometimes referred to by players as "cursed" blocks. These are often out-of-place blocks that you can spot pretty easily. For example, one Adventure has four glazed terracotta blocks you must collect to stop skeletons from spawning. In general, if mobs keep respawning, look out for special blocks that are different from most of the other blocks in the build and break them.

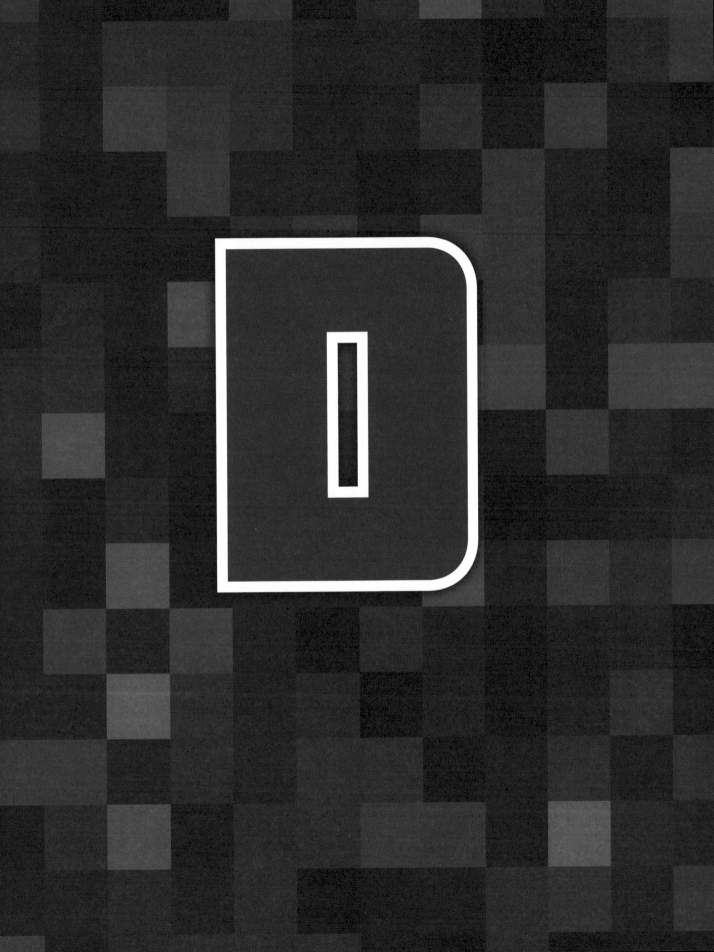

DAILY CHALLENGES

Every day you'll get a new set of challenges you can access from the Trophy icon on the sidebar. They're pretty easy, and usually consist of two collecting challenges (e.g., collect one epic tappable) and two buildplate challenges (e.g., place two mobs on a buildplate).

DANDELIONS

Dandelions are a small yellow flower found in most Minecraft biomes and you use them to craft yellow dye. You can get them from Grass and Pond tappables and find them in Adventures and buildplates.

DARK OAK LEAVES

Dark oak leaves are the block that creates the canopy of the dark oak tree. Like Oak leaves, they have a chance of dropping an apple (or stick or sapling) when they decay or are broken. You can get the leaf block if you use shears; otherwise, when they decay or break, they will disappear.

DARK OAK LOGS

Dark oak logs are blocks that form the trunk of the dark oak tree. You can use them as fuel, right-click them with an axe to create stripped dark oak logs, craft them into planks, and you can find them in some Adventures and buildplates.

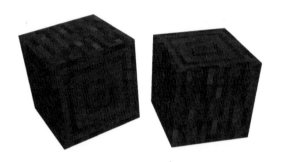

DARK OAK SAPLINGS

To grow a dark oak tree, you will need dark oak saplings. You can get these from decaying leaves of a dark oak tree.

DARK OAK TREES

Dark oak trees are native to the Dark Forest biome, and in Minecraft Earth, you can find them in some Adventures and buildplates. Their trunks are 2x2 square and they have a wide canopy that creates dark shadowy areas. You do need four dark oak saplings to grow a dark oak tree, and it can be difficult to get many saplings from the leaves of dark oak trees.

DARK OAK WOOD PLANKS

Dark oak planks are crafted from dark oak logs and are a popular building material. You can use them as fuel, as planks for any recipe requiring wood planks, and to create dark oak buttons, pressure plates, doors, trapdoors, fences, gates, stairs, and slabs.

DEAD BUSH

A dead bush is a decorative plant that you can find primarily in Minecraft's dryer biomes. When you break the plant block, it may drop sticks; if you use shears you can retrieve the dead bush item. You can find them in some Adventures and buildplates.

DEFENSE BOOST

The Defense boost will lower the attack damage done to you by enemy strikes in an Adventure. Level I decreases the damage by 25% for 10 minutes, Level II by 50% for 15 minutes, and Level III by 75% for 30 minutes. The corresponding toy mini-figures that give a defense boost (Level I strength) are "Defending Alex" and "Enraged Golem."

DETECTOR RAIL

Detector rails are a special type of rail. When a minecart rides over a detector rail, the detector rail emits a redstone signal that can be used to power other redstone components or functional blocks. For example, the detector rail's signal could be used to light up a redstone lamp as a cart passes over it. You can craft detector rails from iron, a stone pressure plate, and redstone; you can find them in Adventure chests and in some Adventures.

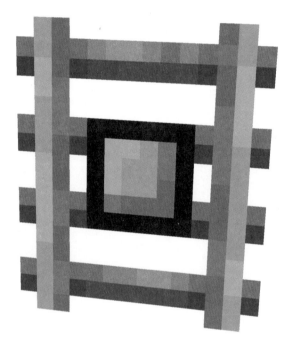

DIAMOND

Diamonds are the precious prize of mining—they're top-of-the-line material for creating durable, fast, and strong weapons and tools. You can find them rarely in some Adventures, as well as in loot from some rarer Adventure chests. You will need an iron pickaxe or higher to mine diamond ore, and this diamond ore drops diamond items. You can craft shiny blue

diamond blocks from 9 diamonds, and smelt diamond ore into single diamonds.

DIAMOND ORE

Diamond ore is the source, of course, for Minecraft's precious diamond gems. Veins of typically 1–3 diamond ore can be found in some Adventures, and you will need an iron pick or better to mine the ore, which will drop diamonds. You can also get some diamonds as loot from Adventure chests.

DIORITE

Diorite is a type of stone that you will find underground in Minecraft. It has a whitish, speckled appearance and is often the loser of block beauty pageants although it is quite possible to create beautiful builds with this block. You can craft it into stairs or steps as well as polished diorite blocks and slabs. You can also make diorite by crafting nether quartz with cobblestone. You can find it in Stone tappables, and mine it from some buildplates and Adventures.

DIRT

Dirt blocks are often found just beneath a top layer of grass in Minecraft landscapes, and if you cover grass blocks with other blocks, they will turn into dirt blocks. They are a great block to use as temporary, placeholder blocks when you are building because they can be broken pretty quickly. Dirt blocks placed next to grass blocks will eventually convert to grass blocks, as the grass "spreads." You can plant trees, flowers, and other plants on dirt. You can find dirt in Grass and Pond tappables as well as Adventures and buildplates.

DOORS

There are seven types of door in Minecraft. Six are crafted from the six types of wood planks and the iron door is crafted from iron ingots. Wood doors can only be opened by players or by a redstone pulse. Iron doors can only be opened with a redstone pulse—usually a button or pressure plate is used. Oak doors can be found in Chest tappables, and doors in general can be found in buildplates and Adventures.

DROPS

Drops are items that are generated when a mob is killed; they fall as items on the blocks beneath the mob. For example, a skeleton can drop bones, arrows, and bows, and a chicken drops feathers and raw chicken. The word drops also refers to the drops from blocks when you mine or break them, especially when the broken block gives you something other than that block. For example, a gravel block sometimes drops flint when you break it.

DYES

There are sixteen dyes in Minecraft, and these can be crafted used to create colored versions of those blocks. You can dye beds, concrete powder, glass blocks, sheep, terracotta, and wool.

Dye	Made from	
White	Bone meal	
Light Gray	Azure bluets, Oxeye daisies, White tulips, black dye and two white dye, gray dye and one white dye.	
Gray	White dye and black dye	
Black	Ink sacs from squid	
Brown	Cocoa beans	
Red	Beetroot, poppies, red tulips, rose bushes	
Orange	Orange tulips, red and yellow dye	
Yellow	Dandelions, sunflowers	
Lime	Green dye and white dye	
Green	Cactus (smelting)	
Cyan	Blue dye and green dye	
Light blue	Blue orchids, blue dye and white dye	
Blue	Lapis, cornflowers	
Purple	Red and blue dye	
Magenta	Lilacs, red dye and blue dye and white dye, purple dye and pink dye, pink dye and red dye and blue dye.	
Pink	Peonies, pink tulips, red and white dye	

57

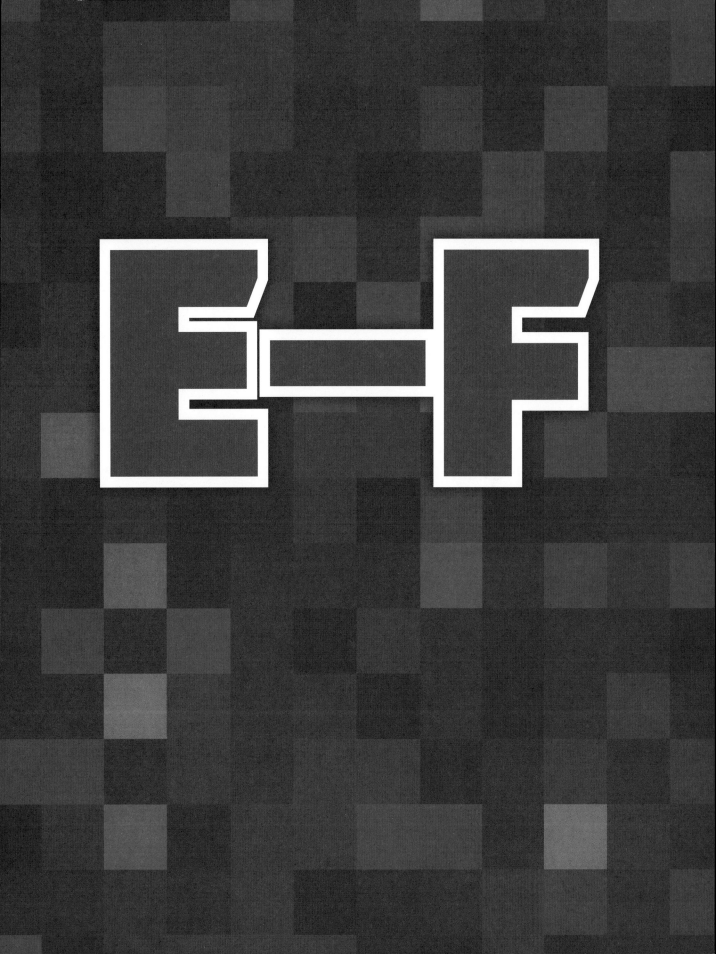

EGG

Chickens can lay eggs! Throw an egg against the ground or a block and it will break, with a chance of spawning a chick! You can also get eggs from Chicken tappables and common Adventure chests.

ENTITIES

Entities are objects in Minecraft that can move: mobs like sheep and skeletons, projectiles like snowballs and arrows, and other moving blocks, like minecarts.

EQUIPMENT

Equipment is the category used in Minecraft Earth's recipes, inventories, and journal to display not just weapons and tools, but also food, which is a necessity for restoring your health during combat in Adventures. If you're having difficulty finding food items, look for the equipment category's icon, the sword.

EXPERIENCE

As you collect tappables, complete Adventures, and fulfill challenges, you'll also collect experience points. As you gain more experience, you also move up in levels of experience. Each experience level (from 1 to 25) requires an increasing number of experience points (XP) to get to the next level—you need many more experience points to jump from level 24 to 25 than you do from level 1 to level 2.

Experience points in the game look like neon green blobs—here you'll get 85 of them for completing a Tappable challenge.

FARMING

Farming is the art of growing food and resource crops in Minecraft Earth. For most crops you will need to create farmland in order to grow them. You use seeds to plant some crops like beetroots. For others, like potatoes, you use the plant item itself. In addition to food crops, players also create farms for sugarcane, cactus, cocoa beans, melons, pumpkins, and mushrooms.

FARMLAND

Farmland is a special block needed to farm many crops, and you create it by using a hoe on dirt or grass. However, unwatered farmland can eventually revert to dirt. To water farmland, make sure that each block of farmland is within 4 blocks of a block of water. A common tactic to handle this is to create a 9 by 9 block area of farmland, with the center block being water. You can also break growing plants and return farmland to dirt by jumping on the farmland block.

FENCE

In Minecraft, players and mobs can jump up single blocks; fences prevent this. You can confine mobs like cows and sheep to fenced-in areas. To get into a fenced-in area, you can place a fence gate between two fence blocks. There are fences for each type of wood.

FERN

Ferns are a common Minecraft plant often found in the Taiga biome, and you can find them in Grass and Pond tappables and many buildplates and Adventures. A variant, the large fern, is rarer and can be found in the Rangers Rest buildplate.

You can find both small and large ferns.

FLECKED SHEEP

This fuzzy brown sheep will give you brown wool if you shear it, and drop raw mutton and wool if you kill it. You can find it in Sheep tappables. [Health: 8]

FLINT

Flint is a material that you can get in Stone tappables; and it is also sometimes dropped by gravel blocks when you break them (a shovel is best). You use flint to make flint and steel.

FLINT AND STEEL

Flint and steel is a tool you use to set things alight, like TNT, and you craft it from an iron ingot and a piece of flint.

FLOWER POT

You can craft a flower pot with three single bricks, and you can place flowers, sapling, and other plants, like ferns, cactus, mushrooms and bamboo in them as a decoration. You can find flower pots in Chest tappables, some Adventure chests, and in Adventures and buildplates.

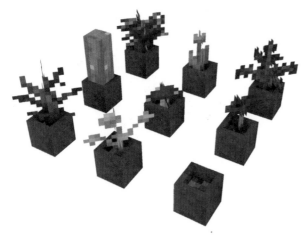

Flowerpots can hold more than flowers; you can use them for cactus, dead bushes, ferns, saplings, even mushrooms.

FLOWERS

Flowers in Minecraft may be one or two blocks high. Small (one-block high) flowers include Azure Bluets, Blue Orchids, Buttercups, Cornflowers, Dandelions, Lilacs, lilies of the valley, Poppies, Tulips (Pink, Orange, Red, White). Tall (two blocks high) flowers, often called double-tall, or two-high plants include Lilacs, Peonies, Rose Bushes, and Sunflowers.

You can place flowers in flower pots for decoration, and you can grow flowers from grass blocks by using bone meal on the grass block. You can also use bone meal on a double-tall flower and this will produce a second flower in its item form. Flowers are used to create dye. You can find flowers in Grass and Pond tappables and Adventures and buildplates.

FOOD

The foods of Minecraft Earth are what replenish your health when you are damaged in combat. In an Adventure, you can take damage from mobs like skeletons shooting at you and zombies attacking you. Foods can come from food crops, like potatoes and carrots, or meats, dropped from farm animals like cows and sheep, and many of these foods can be cooked in a furnace to give even more nutritional value. The foods of Minecraft aren't created equal: some restore more health points (HP) when you eat them.

FOOD BOOST

If you don't have much food for regenerating health during an Adventure, you might want to try a Food Boost, purchasable through the Store for rubies. This will increase the amount of health regeneration eating a food gives you. A Level I Food Boost replenishes 10% more health and lasts 10 minutes; Level II gives you 20% more for 15 minutes; and a Level III replenishes 30% more for 30 minutes. You can also get a Level I–strength food boost from the toy mini-figure, "Fishing Polar Bear."

FUEL

To smelt items in a furnace, you will need a source of fuel to add to the furnace. This can be wood logs, planks, and other wood items, coal, charcoal, or a bucket of lava. Different fuel types burn for longer than other types, and you will typically have a lot more wooden items to use as fuel or convert into charcoal than you will coal.

Along with coal and charcoal, you can use a host of other materials as fuel for your furnace, including old wooden tools, when you open up the fuel interface before smelting.

FURNACE

In Minecraft, furnaces are blocks that use fuel to smelt some resources and turn them into other resources (like cactus into green dye), cook food (turning raw mutton into cooked mutton), and to smelt ores (turning iron ore into iron ingots). In Minecraft Earth, you don't need to craft a furnace; you use a virtual furnace in the Make Stuff > Smelting area.

FURNACE GOLEM

The furnace golem is a neutral mob that attacks hostile mobs on sight. It looks as if it has been welded together from several furnaces and its mighty arm swings can both set its targets on fire as well as send them air-bound. They'll drop coal and iron nuggets when killed, and you can find them in Stone tappables. They will occasionally hand a Mob of Me a torch as a gift. [Health: 100]

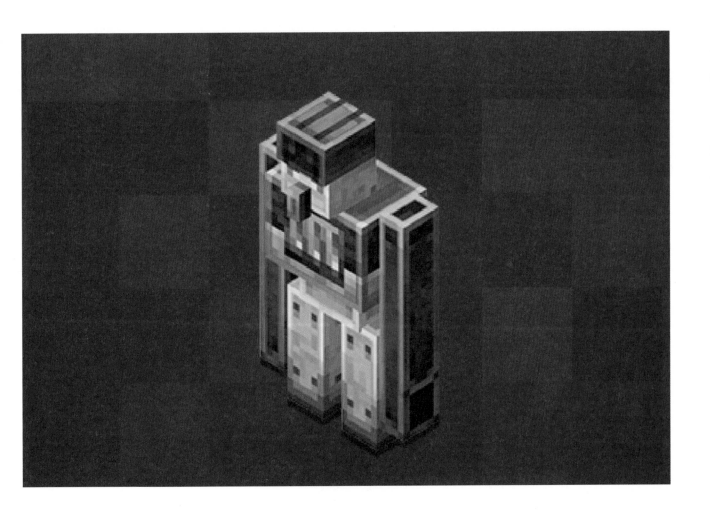

GATE

Gates are doors for fences, and you can place them between two fence blocks to allow access into a fenced in area. As with fences, you can't jump over them, even though they are only one block high. Gates can be opened and shut with redstone power. Gates can be made of any wood plank type, and you can find them in Adventures and Buildplates. You can find oak gates in Chest tappables.

You can make gates using any of the Minecraft woods.

GLASS BLOCKS

Glass blocks are a transparent, decorative building block that you create by smelting sand in a furnace. Once smelted, you can dye 8 glass blocks at a time with any of the 16 dyes. Because glass blocks and pane break (and disappear) when you break them, use Pick Up mode in buildplates to pick them up.

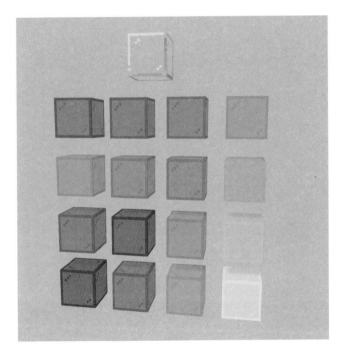

Plain glass (top) can be colored using any of the 16 dyes.

GLASS PANES

Glass panes are transparent decorative blocks that are thin like real glass panes in window. You craft 16 panes them from 6 regular or dyed glass blocks. Two glass panes will attach to each other and to neighboring blocks, and they are often used to create windows and chandeliers.

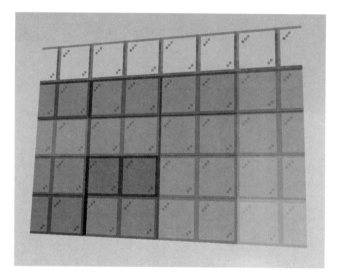

A row of plain glass panes at the top, above colored panes crafted from dyed glass blocks.

GLAZED TERRACOTTA

Glazed terracotta is a decorative block that is made by smelting dyed terracotta. There are sixteen colors of glazed terracotta, and each has a different pattern. The blocks are designed so that the pattern's position rotates depending on which direction you face while you place it. You can make different 2x2 block patterns with each glazed terracotta type (color) by facing in different directions as you place the blocks. For example, one way to make a 2x2 pattern is to change direction in a clockwise fashion as you place the four blocks: First face North, then East, then South, then West.

Each color of glazed terracotta can be made into several patterns, depending on which way you face when placing the individual blocks.

GLOW SQUID

What has 8 arms and glows in the dark? It's a glow squid, which you can occasionally find in Pond tappables and see in some Adventures. Place it in a pond on a buildplate to see it shine. If you ever had the need to kill it, it would drop a few ink sacs. [Health: 10]

GLOWSTONE

Glowstone is a block found in the original game's Nether (hell-like or underworld) biome. It emits light and is often used as a decorative

block as well as a replacement for torches. Breaking glowstone will drop several glowstone dust, and you can craft glowstone bocks from four dust.

GLOWSTONE DUST

Glowstone dust is a crafting resource in Minecraft, and is used to make light-emitting glowstone blocks. You can find it in Chest tappables and some Adventure chests.

GOLD

Gold is a valuable and rare metal in Minecraft that you get from mining and then smelting gold ore. Although it is not very durable, and not a good choice in general for tools and weapons, it is used to craft special items like powered rails and golden carrots—the best and most expensive food sources in the game. The gold ingots that you get from smelting gold ore can be crafted into gold blocks or into gold nuggets. You can find gold in Adventure chests.

GOLD ORE

Gold ore is found in small veins in Adventures. You will need and iron or better pickaxe to mine it, and it will drop gold ore blocks that need to be smelted into ingots.

GOLDEN CARROT

Golden carrots are the best health-replenishing and one of the most expensive foods in Minecraft. You'll need 8 gold nuggets (crafted from gold ingots) and a carrot to make one golden carrot that will restore 10 health points.

GOLEMS

Golems are a unique Minecraft mob: They are neutral mobs that offer aid to players and passive mobs by attacking hostile mobs. Golems in real life are a mythical, anthropomorphic (human-like) creature from Jewish folklore, said to be formed from clay or mud and then brought to life, usually to perform service or work. Minecraft has iron golems, spawned in villages to protect their inhabitants, and snow golems, created from snow and pumpkin heads. Minecraft Earth has several unique and new golems, like the Furnace golem and Melon golems.

This iron golem (from Minecraft) pictured on a Minecraft Earth alert protects villagers from hostile mobs.

GRANITE

Granite is a stone type that you will find underground in patches. It has a reddish-white texture, and like other stone variants, can be crafted into stairs, polished granite blocks, stairs, and slabs. You can craft granite blocks from diorite and nether quartz. You can also find granite blocks in Stone tappables, Adventures, and buildplates.

GRASS

Grass is a plant you'll find growing on grass blocks. It can be small (one block high) or tall (two-block high). You can grow grass on grass blocks by using bone meal on that block. Additionally, you can grow small grass into a tall grass by using bone meal. You must use shears to break and collect grass items. You can find grass in Grass and Pond tappables and in buildplates and Adventures.

GRASS BLOCK

Grass blocks are like dirt blocks but with a layer of grassy green on their top surface, and you can add bone meal to them to grow grass (plant blocks) and flowers on them. Grass blocks will also spread to nearby dirt blocks (but not coarse dirt), converting them to grass blocks. Placing another block on top of a grass block, will, after a while, return the grass block to dirt. You can also use a hoe on a grass block to change it into farmland and right-click a shovel on grass to change it into a path block. When you break a grass block, it turns into a dirt block, unless you use Pick Up mode on a buildplate. You can find grass blocks in buildplates and Adventures.

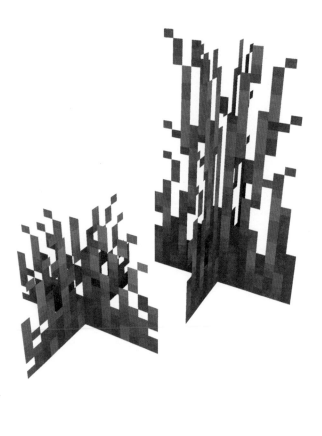

GRASS TAPPABLE

Grass tappables are one of the three "mound" tappables, along with Pond and Stone tappables that you'll find on the World Map. Tap them to collect one to three goodies, which may be acacia saplings, coarse dirt, cocoa beans, creepers, dirt, ferns, flowers, grass, gravel, harelequin rabbits, jungle saplings, jumbo rabbits, lily pads, melon golems, melon seeds, muddy rabbits, pumpkins, pumpkin seeds, red mushrooms, vested rabbits, and wheat seeds.

GRAVEL

Gravel is one of the few blocks in Minecraft that is affected by gravity and you can break it most easily with a shovel. It must be placed on another block, or it will fall. It is found often underground or in river beds. You use gravel with sand (and a dye) to create concrete powder. You can find gravel in Grass tappables, Pond tappables, Adventures, and buildplates.

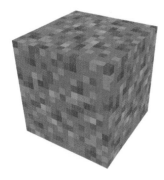

GUNPOWDER

Gunpowder is a crafting resource that you use to make TNT. It is a drop from creepers, and you can find it in Chest tappables and Adventure chests.

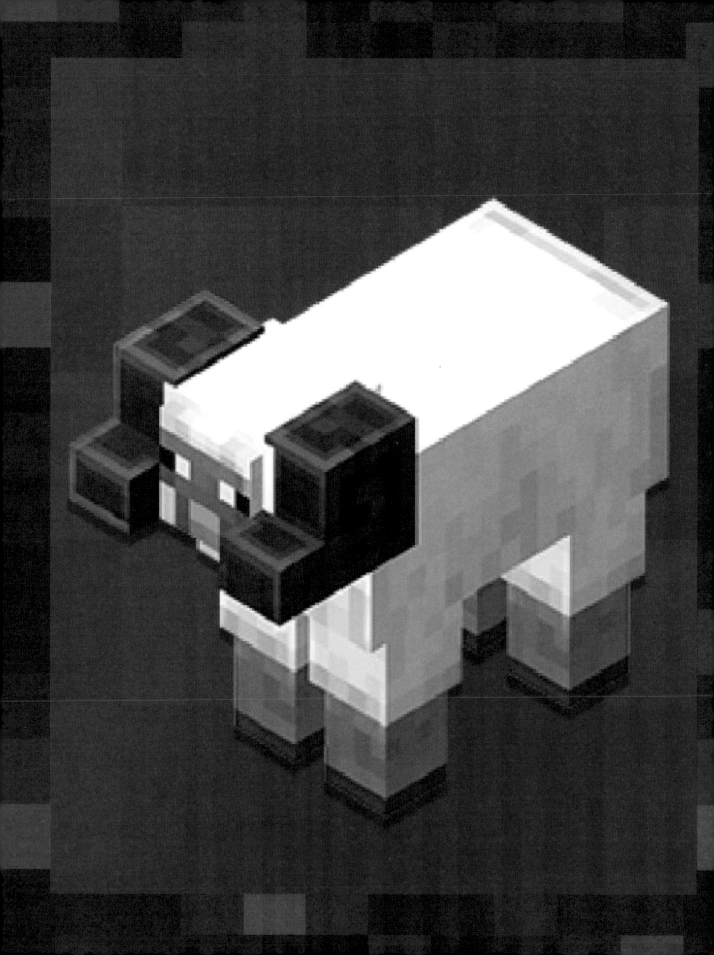

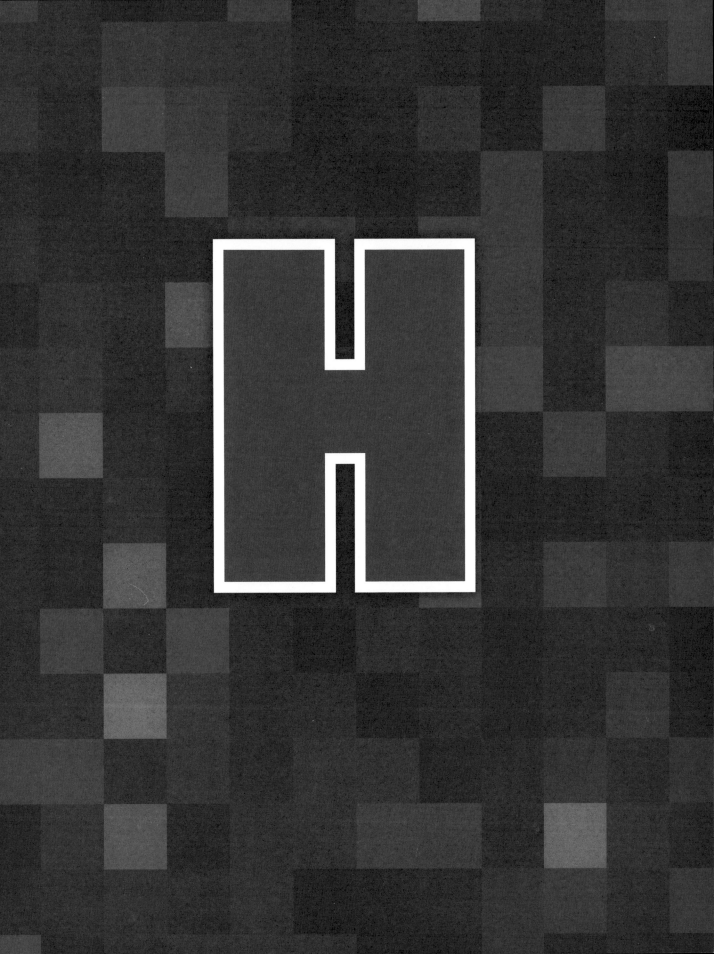

HARELEQUIN RABBIT

The Harelequin rabbit (yes, "hare" lequin!) is a rare rabbit variant that is colored white, black, and a rich brown. You'll find it in Grass and Pond tappables. [Health: 3]

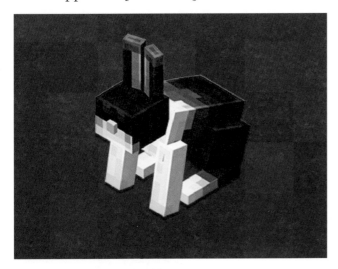

HEALTH BAR

Your health bar displays at the top of your World Map screen beside your Profile icon, and it shows you how much health you have. When it's full, you're at full health. When you take damage (such as being shot by a skeleton),

your health decreases and so does your red health bar. You can only take damage during an Adventure, and you can only replenish your health by eating. As a player, you have 20 health points, and other mobs are assigned health points (HP) as well.

HEALTH BOOST

The Health Boost ups the maximum health in your Health bar, meaning anyone attacking you won't have it so easy. Levels I, II, and III up your health by 10%, 20%, and 30% respectively. You can also use the toy mini-figures "Healing Witch," "Regenerating Mooshroom," and "Snacking Rabbit" for a Level I strength Health boost.

HOARDING BOOST

The Hoarding boost will keep your backpack contents safe if you die in an Adventure (to keep your hotbar contents, you'll need the Keeper Boost). Level I lasts for 10 minutes, Level II for 15 minutes, and Level III for 30 minutes. The toy mini-figure that will give you a Level I strength Hoarding boost is the "Hoarding Skeleton."

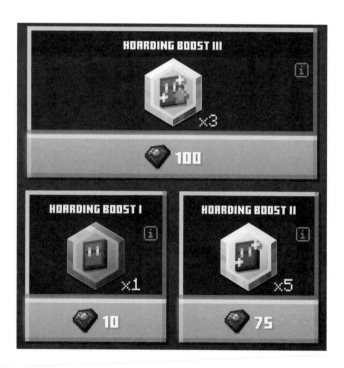

HOE

A hoe is a tool you use to prepare land for farming, and right-clicking a Minecraft hoe on grass or dirt will turn that block into farmland that you can place crops on.

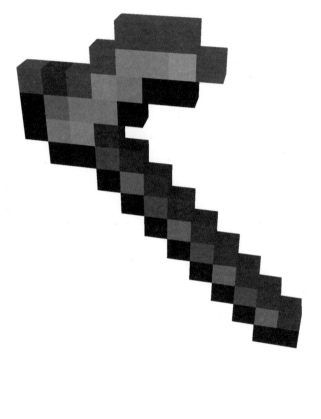

HORNED SHEEP

The horned sheep is the rarest of Minecraft Earth sheep variants, and it isn't happy. It is a neutral, not passive mob, and will fight back any enemy using its horns. It will also occasionally attack other horned sheep. It drops wool, raw mutton, and horns when killed, and you can find it in Sheep tappables. [Health: 8; Damage: 3]

HOTBAR

Your hotbar is the row of inventory items at the bottom of your screen that appears when you open your inventory or start an Adventure or buildplate. When you place blocks or use tools and weapons, you can only use the objects stored in your hotbar. If you want to use something that is not in your hotbar, you'll have to move it from your inventory to your hotbar. (Click in the inventory and then click in the space you want to place it in your hotbar.) In an Adventure, you only have access to your hotbar, and a temporary backpack that opens to store extra materials; in a buildplate, you can still open up and manage your inventory.

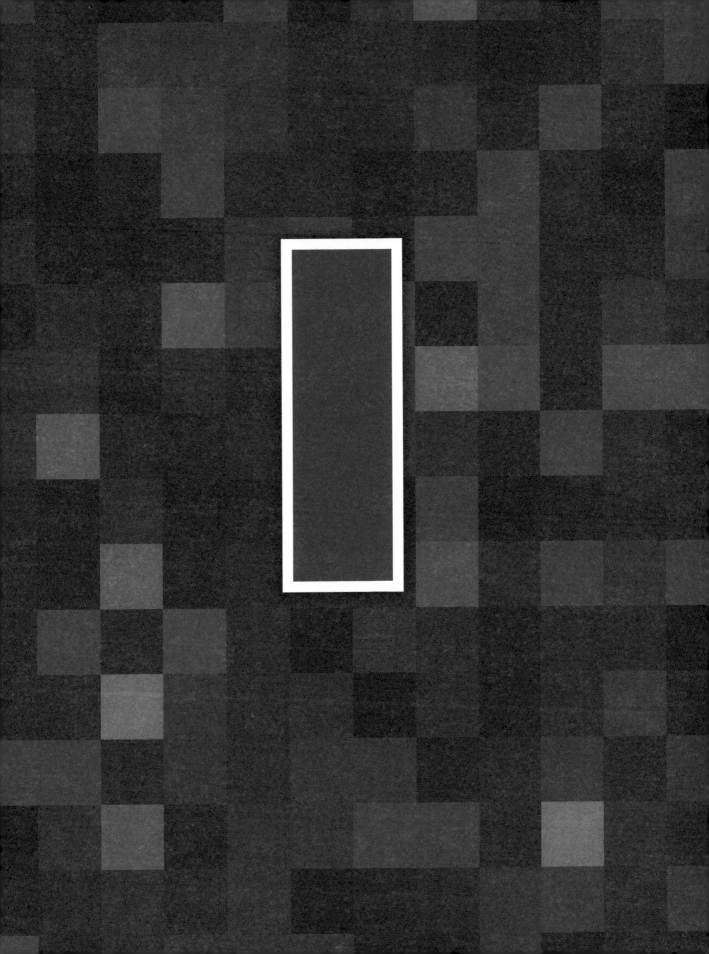

ICE

Ice blocks in Minecraft will form out of water blocks that are in frozen biomes, like the Snowy Tundra biome. (To do so, the water block must be exposed to the sky and be next to a non-water block.) Ice blocks are slippery to walk on and will melt if they are near a heat or a light source like a torch or glowstone. Ice will disappear when you break it, so use Pick Up mode on a buildplate to handle it. You can find ice in Adventures and buildplates.

You'll see the "I for information button" in various places in the game, like the inventory. Click on it to find out more information about the item in your inventory, or the current game element.

INK SAC

Ink sacs are items dropped by squid and glow squid when you kill them, and they are the only source of black dye in the game. You can find them in Chest tappables.

INFORMATION BUTTON

INKY SHEEP

The Inky sheep isn't fully covered in an inky black coat as you might expect: it has dark limbs and underbelly, and dark stripes on its head. You can find it in Sheep tappables. [Health: 8]

INTERACT MODE

Interact mode allows you to interact with blocks and tools on a buildplate in a classic Minecraft survival way. You won't be able to pick up a block by clicking it, you'll have to use the right tool for it. You will be able to interact with things like buttons and levers, and use shears on a sheep.

INVENTORY

Your inventory is where you store the stuff—blocks, items, weapons, tools, even mobs—that you collect as you play Adventures, complete challenges, and tap tappables. To open the inventory, just click the Inventory button on the bottom menu on your World Map. As you collect, stuff automagically transports to your inventory—first to your hotbar, if you have any

slots open, and then to your inventory. Your hotbar, a row of 7 slots at the bottom of your Inventory. Your Inventory and hotbar shows on Buildplates but only your hotbar is usable during Adventures. You can sort and filter your inventory in various ways, as well as search for specific items. You can also move items back and forth from your main inventory to your hotbar.

IRON

Besides diamond, iron is the strongest and most durable metal in Minecraft, and is a great choice for weapons and tools. You get iron ingots from smelting iron ore that you mine in Adventures. You can also craft iron blocks and iron nuggets from the ingots, and iron is used in a number of other recipes, such as iron doors, iron bars, and more. Iron ore can be found in Adventures

and in the Hearth Home buildplate, and you can get iron ingots from Adventure chests and as rare drops from zombies.

IRON ORE

Iron ore can be found in small veins in Adventures, often hidden behind other blocks or features.

ITEMS

You'll hear the word "items" often used to describe the non-blocky stuff in Minecraft that isn't placed down like a block: tools and weapons, for example. Technically, items are anything that can appear in an inventory or your hand. Some items, like a flowerpot, can be placed down like a block and have a block form. Likewise, blocks, when they are in your hand, are also in their item form.

J-K-L

JOLLY LLAMA

The Jolly Llama is a brown and white llama festooned in holiday gear: reindeer antlers, a collar with gold bells, and a green carpet with red fringe. It hops about, and eating ferns will make it especially happy. It is found in rare holiday-only buildplates. If you kill it (would you, really?), it will drop a little leather. [Health: 15 to 30]

JOURNAL

The Journal keeps track of every item, block, and mob you've collected so far. When you find a new block in an Adventure, on a buildplate, or from a tappable, or win it in a challenge, a little virtual sticker for it is placed on in your journal. Access your journal by clicking the journal icon on the sidebar. You can sort through your collection, filter it, and the outlines of missing items will show you what you have left to collect. You can also claim some rewards for filling out your journal.

JUMBO RABBIT

It's a big brown rabbit! You can get the unusually large Jumbo rabbit from Grass and Pond tappables and find it in some Adventures. It can drop rabbit hide, raw rabbit meat, and sometimes a rabbit's foot, if you kill it. [Health: 3]

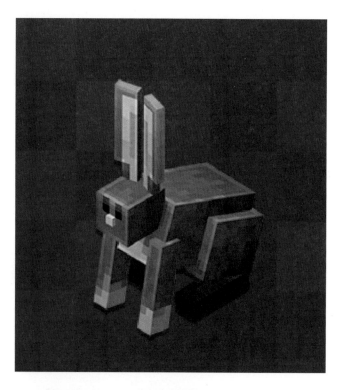

blocks have a chance of dropping 1–2 sticks or a sapling.

JUNGLE LOGS

Jungle tree logs make up the blocks used for the jungle tree. They have a somewhat striped appearance. You can use an axe on a jungle tree log to create a stripped (of its bark) log. You can find them in Adventures and in buildplates.

JUNGLE LEAVES

Jungle leaves are the block used to create the canopy of a jungle tree. They have a distinctive pattern that evokes wider leaves of tropical and subtropical plants. As with other leaf blocks, you can use shears on them to drop the actual leaf block. Broken or decaying jungle leaf

JUNGLE TREE

One of the six trees of Minecraft (acacia, birch, dark oak, jungle, oak, and spruce), jungle oaks have a distinctive, somewhat stripy bark. You can grow them from single jungle saplings, or you can grow a mega jungle tree by placing four saplings in a square. The large jungle trees can reach over 30 blocks high. In the wild [of Minecraft], cocoa beans and vines grow on the largest Jungle trees; in fact, you will need jungle logs in order to grow cocoa beans. You can find jungle logs in buildplates and Adventures and jungle saplings in Grass and Pond tappables.

JUNGLE TREE SAPLINGS

To grow a jungle tree, you will need to plant its sapling. This will grow a jungle tree; you can grow a large jungle tree by planting four saplings in a 2x2 square. You can find jungle saplings in Grass and Pond tappables.

JUNGLE WOOD PLANKS

Four jungle tree planks are created by crafting one jungle tree log. You can use planks in a number of recipes asking for wood, as well as create jungle wood buttons, doors, trapdoors, fences, gates, stairs, and slabs.

KEEPER BOOST

When you die in an Adventure, you lose all the contents of your hotbar (and your backpack). You can prevent this by activating a Keeper Boost, which will save all your hotbar goodies. Keeper Boost Level I lasts for 10 minutes, Level II lasts for 15 minutes, and Level III lasts half an hour. You can also get a Level I strength boost with the Minecraft Earth mini-figure toy, "Undying Evoker."

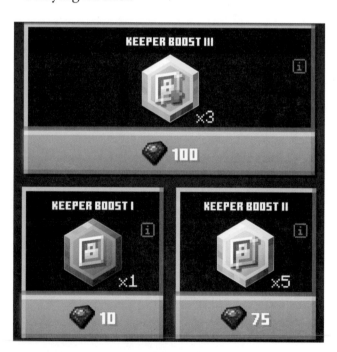

LAPIS LAZULI

Lapis lazuli (usually referred to as lapis) is a Minecraft ore used for making blue dye, and in Minecraft proper, for enchanting. You can craft decorative lapis blocks from 9 lapis. You can get lapis from mining lapis ore (you'll need an iron or diamond pick) in Adventures, and you can also find it in some Adventure chests.

LAPIS LAZULI ORE

You can find lapis lazuli ore in small veins in Minecraft Adventures, often hidden by other blocks or build features. Mine it with an iron or diamond pickaxe to get its drop of the lapis lazuli gem.

LAVA

Lava is kind of a big deal in Minecraft, where it is much more common than in real life. Lava often collects in pools not far underground and sometimes even aboveground. It may ooze down the sides of cave walls, and touching it will set you alight for a short time. A single lava source will flow slowly for several blocks, and it can destroy items and plants in its path. You can pick the lava source up, and place it down, with a bucket. If flowing lava touches water, it forms cobblestone; if it touches water on the top surface of a water source block it will form stone. And if water is poured over lava, the lava will turn into obsidian.

LEATHER

Leather is a crafting resource you can get as drops from cows. You can also craft it from four rabbit hides.

LEAVES

Leaves are blocks that are used to create the canopy of trees, and each tree type has its own unique leaf block. The color of leaf blocks (except for spruce and birch) change when the tree is in a different biome. Leaf blocks that were created as part of a tree will despawn or decay when they are no longer within 6 blocks of another leaf block or log. To collect a leaf block, you use a shear; any other tool will cause it to disappear. Use a hoe to break leaves quickly. When leaf blocks are destroyed, they have a chance of dropping a sapling or stick. Oak and dark oak leaves also have a chance of dropping an apple. Leaf blocks are great decorative blocks for creating custom tree and plants.

When you chop down a tree, like this oak tree, its leaf blocks will gradually decay, or despawn.

LEVERS

Levers are redstone components like switches, with an on state and off state. In their "on" state they emit a constant, full-strength (15) redstone power signal. You can turn them off

to stop the signal. They can power an adjacent solid block, including a redstone mechanism component (like a piston), or redstone dust.

You can craft them from a stick and a cobblestone block, and you may find them in Chest tappables and in some Adventures.

LILAC

The lilac is a tall light purplish-pink flower that you can craft into magenta dye. Its natural home in Minecraft is in the forested biomes, and you can find it in some Adventures and buildplates.

LILY OF THE VALLEY

The lily of the valley, like the lilac, is a plant that grows in Minecraft's forested biomes. You

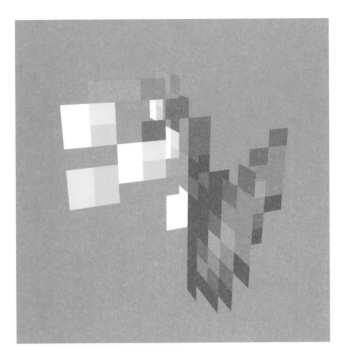

can get lilies of the valley from Grass and Pond tappables, and find them in some Adventures and buildplates.

LILY PADS

Lily pads are handy plants for decorating ponds, and they can also be useful if you want to start building in the middle of a pond, lake

or ocean—you can place the lily pad down on water and then place another block above it. You can also use them to make walkable pathways on top of water. You can find them in Grass and Pond tappables as well as a very few Adventures and buildplates.

LOGS

Logs are the blocks tree trunks are made from, and each tree type (acacia, birch, dark oak, jungle, oak, and spruce) has differently colored logs. Use an axe to chop them quickly. They're used as decorative building blocks and you can craft them into plank blocks, which are used for many more crafting recipes.

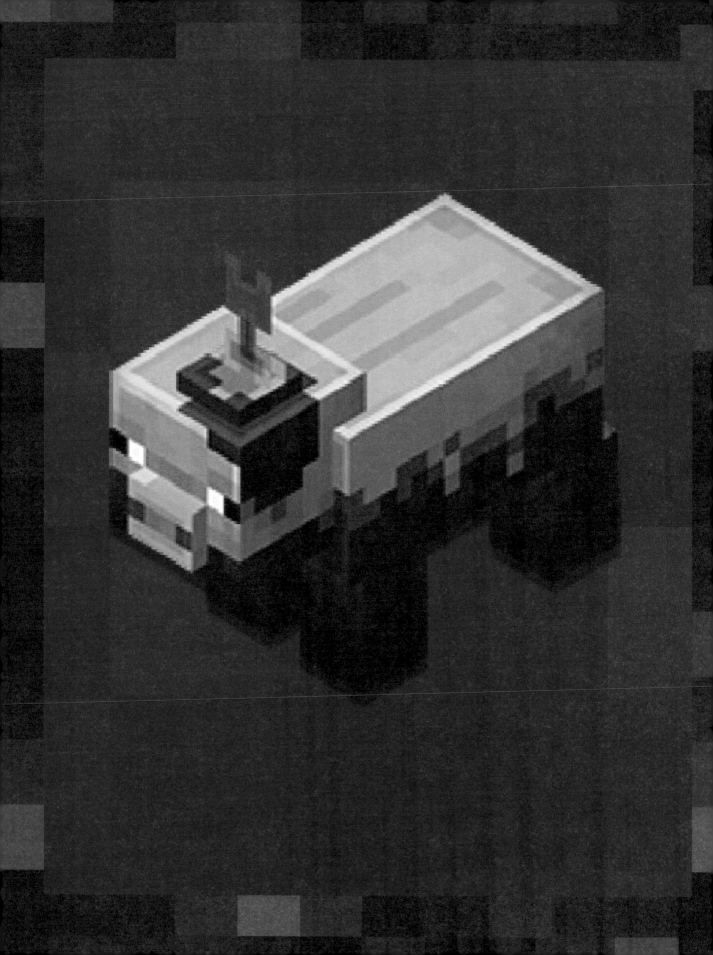

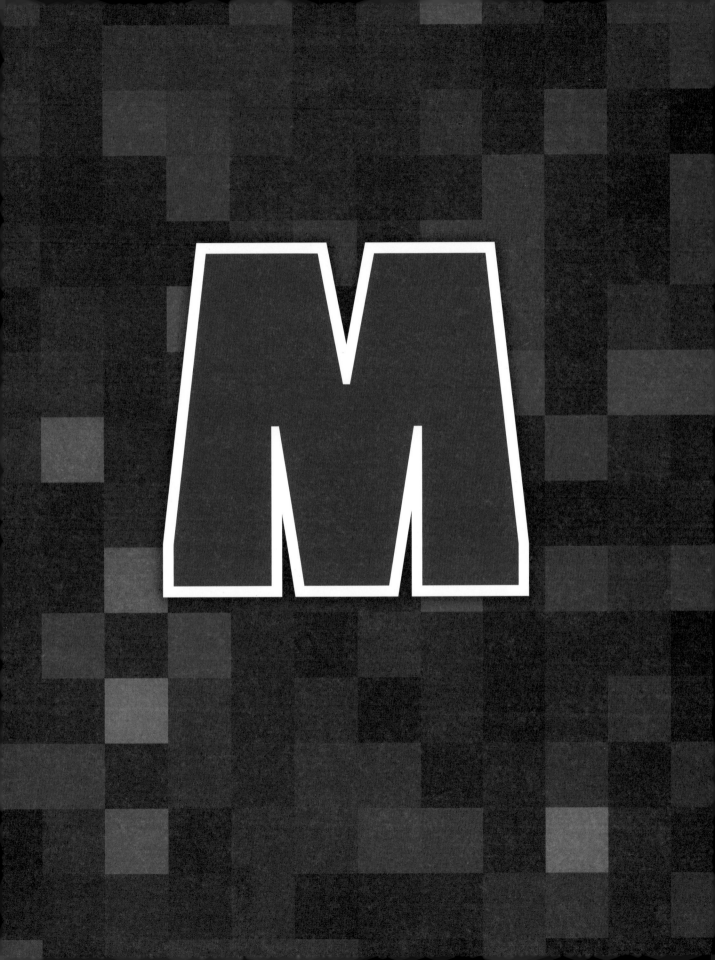

MELONS

In Minecraft, melons are a jungle fruit and when you harvest them they will give 3 to 7 melon slices to eat. They're one of the few fruit, along with pumpkins, that you only need to seed once. They first grow a stalk, and when the stalk is mature, a melon fruit will grow on the block next to it. Melon seeds should be grown on watered farmland. At least one block next to the stalk should be some type of dirt block, like grass or dirt, for the melon to grow on. You can craft 9 melon slices to re-create a melon block. You can find melons in Adventures and a few buildplates, and you can find melon seeds in Grass and Pond tappables and in common Adventure chests.

MELON GOLEMS

The Melon Golem acts as a helpful ally in battling hostile mobs, spitting a slew of melon seeds at the enemy. Despite this horrifying assault technique, the melon golem itself is rather weak and is often better used in groups. Also, it looks like a snowperson with a melon head and stick arms and leaves a trail of snow behind it. You can find melon golems in Grass and Pond tappables. They drop melon slices upon death. [Health: 4]

MIDNIGHT CHICKEN

The Midnight chicken is a dark blue, purplish chicken you can get from Chicken tappables. [Health: 4]

MINECART

Minecarts are entity blocks that can move along on top of rails and given a boost of power through a powered rail. They can also be pushed along flat ground. Most mobs can be placed in minecarts by being pushed into them.

MINECOINS

Minecoins are an in game currency that you use primarily in the Character Creator area, where you can purchase costumes and costume parts from the Minecraft Marketplace used by Bedrock and Console Minecraft editions. Minecoins are shown as a tiny golden coin with an M on them. It will cost you $2 to buy 320 minecoins.

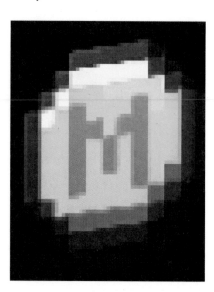

MINING

Mining is how you get blocks make of hard materials, like stone, to break and drop so that you can pick them up and use them elsewhere, for building or as resources to make other blocks. You use a pickaxe to mine these harder blocks, which include many of the blocks found below ground, like stone, granite, andesite, diorite, and ores. Some ores have to be mined with pickaxes made of iron or diamond. If you mine away at a block with the wrong tool, it will (a) take a long time and (b) drop nothing when it breaks.

MINING BOOST

The Mining Boost makes breaking all those blocks with a pickaxe go much faster. Level I increases your mining speed by 25% for 10 minutes; Level II by 50% for 15 minutes; and Level II by 100% for 30 minutes. The mini-figure "Mining Creeper" can also increase your mining speed by 25% for 10 minutes.

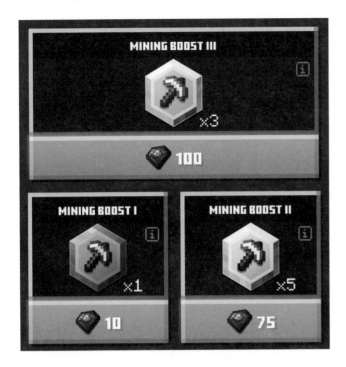

little puff of smoke and may leave behind items or goodies called drops. You also get experience points from killing mobs.

MOB

Mobs, short for "mobile," is the name for moving creatures in Minecraft, from chickens and squid to skeletons and zombies. Mobs are classified as passive (they won't attack you), neutral (they will only attack in some circumstances, such as when you attack them), or hostile (they're always after you!). Mobs are programmed with algorithms called AI that make them behave in specific ways. For example, the AI of a creeper makes it seek out nearby players, follow a path to them, and then explode. Mobs can take damage in various ways, like falling too many blocks, from fire, and being attacked with weapons. They die in a

MOB OF ME

The Mob of Me is a unique and rare mob that is based on your in-game avatar. When you place it on a buildplate, it will take on your skin, and wander about a bit. You can find it as a rare item in Chest tappables and in some Adventures, as well as in several buildplates. [Health: 20]

MOB XP BOOST

The Mob XP Boost ups the amount of experience points (XP) you get when you collect a mob from a tappable. Level I gives you 50% more XP for 10 minutes; Level II gives 75% more for 15 minutes; and Level III doubles (gives you 100% more) for a full 30 minutes. The Minecraft Earth toy mini-figure "Future Chicken Jockey" will also give you 50% more experience for 10 minutes.

MOOBLOOM

Moobloom is another rare Minecraft earth hybrid: a combination cow/buttercup! As it meanders around it will plant a trail of bright buttercups. Like regular cows, the moobloom will drop leather and raw beef when killed, but why would you want to do that? You can find moobloom in Cow tappables and buildplates. [Health: 10]

MOSSY STONE BRICK

Mossy stone bricks are a rare variant of the stone brick block, with a mottled greenish overlay. You can craft them from stone bricks and vines and find them in some Adventures and buildplates. You can also make slabs and stairs with mossy stone bricks.

MUD

Mud is a slow-flowing liquid in Minecraft Earth that some mobs are especially fond of. You can pick mud source blocks up and place them with a bucket. Water flowing over mud will destroy it, and if lava touches flowing mud, it creates dirt.

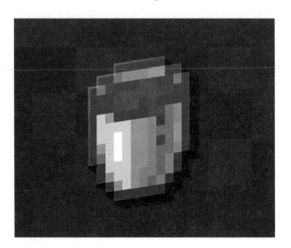

MUDDY PIG

The Muddy pig is unique to Minecraft Earth, and it sports a tulip on its head that drips mud down the side of its face. Its hoofs and belly are also muddy. The Muddy pig will quickly jump into any mud blocks it has access to. You can find Muddy pigs in Pig tappables, as well as some buildplates and Adventures. It drops 1–3 raw pork when killed. [Health: 10]

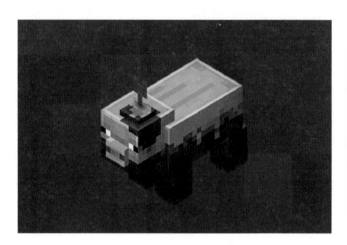

MUDDY RABBIT

The muddy rabbit is a Minecraft Earth rabbit variant that is clearly attracted to patches of mud. You can find it in Grass and Pond tappables. [Health: 3]

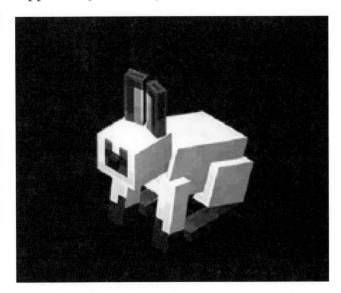

MUSHROOMS

Minecraft has both red and brown mushrooms that you can craft into mushroom stew. They're usually found in low light environments like caves and beneath a forest canopy. You can also find huge mushrooms in Dark Forest biomes alongside dark oaks, which can be broken down into mushroom and mushroom stem blocks that you can use for building. You can find brown mushrooms in Stone tappables, red mushrooms in Grass and Pond tappables, and both types in Adventures and buildplates.

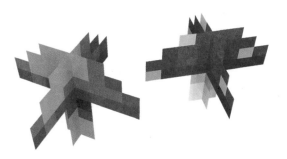

MUSHROOM STEW

You need both types of mushroom, red and brown, plus a wooden bowl, to craft this very hearty and filling stew, which will replenish 8 HP.

N-O

NETHER QUARTZ

Nether quartz is a crafting resource that you can find in Chest tappables and in some Adventure chests. You can use nether quartz to make quartz blocks and redstone comparators.

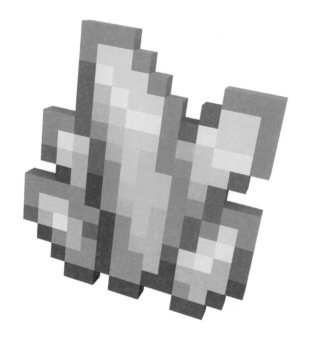

NOTE BLOCK

A note block is a block that sounds a musical note when it is given a redstone pulse. The notes that a note block changes span two octaves in 24 semitones, starting with F#/Gb. You can raise the note a semitone by right-clicking the note block. When you reach the highest note, the note block returns to the lowest tone. Note blocks give different instrument sounds depending on the block they are placed on.

Most blocks will give the note block a piano/harp sound, and other instruments include:

- Banjo (hay bale)
- Bass drum (stone)
- Bell (gold block)
- Chimes (packed ice)
- Flute (clay)
- Didgeridoo (pumpkin)
- Electric piano (glowstone)
- Guitar (wool)
- Iron xylophone (iron block)
- Snare drum (gravel/sand/concrete powder)
- Sticks (glass)
- String bass (wood)
- Xylophone (bone block)

You can chain note blocks together to create a tune with lines of redstone dust. You create

delays between note blocks playing by using redstone repeaters. You craft a note block with wood plank blocks and 1 redstone dust, and you can find them in Chest tappables and common Adventure chests.

OAK LEAVES

Oak leaves are the block that make up the canopy of the oak tree. If you break them (or when they decay after you chop down the oak tree's logs), they have a small chance of dropping a couple of sticks or more rarely an apple. You can shear the leaf blocks to retrieve the actual block of leaves, which you can use as a decoration block.

OAK LOGS

Oak Logs are the blocks that make up the trunk of the oak tree. You'll need an axe to break them quickly. You can use them as a fuel, or as a decorative building block, or craft them into planks. Right-click them with an axe to create a stripped oak log. You can find oak logs in Oak tappables, Adventures, and buildplates.

OAK SAPLINGS

To grow an oak tree, you will need to plant an oak sapling. To make it grow fast, use bone meal on the sapling. You can find oak saplings in Oak tappables and in common Adventure chests.

OAK TAPPABLE

As with other types of tree tappables, Oak tappables can give you logs and saplings. Very rarely, you may also get a spider.

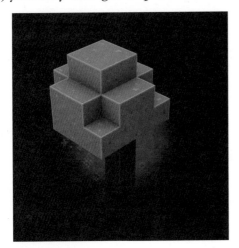

OAK TREE

One of Minecraft's six trees, oak trees are the original Minecraft tree that you punch with your hand (in survival mode, or Adventures, in Minecraft Earth) to get their logs to make your very first tools and weapons. You can find oak trees in buildplates and Adventures.

OAK WOOD PLANKS

Oak wood planks are a decorative building block and resource that you get from crafting oak logs. You can use them in recipes asking for wood, and create oak wood buttons, fences, gates, doors, trapdoors, pressure plates, with them. You can also use them as fuel. You can find oak wood planks in Chest tappables, Adventures, and buildplates.

OCELOTS

Ocelots are wild cats of Minecraft's Jungle biomes. They move quickly and will attack chickens on sight, and creepers are afraid of them. You can find them in the Jungle Treehouse buildplate. They won't drop anything if you kill them. [Health: 10]

P–Q

PACKED ICE

Packed ice is a type of ice that you can find in frozen biomes; it has a slightly deeper blue texture. Unlike regular ice, it won't melt if you put it near light sources, like a torch or glowstone block. You can craft packed ice with 9 regular ice and find it in Adventures and buildplates.

PALE PIG

A light pink version of the traditional Minecraft Pig, the pale pig can be found in Pig tappables. [Health: 10]

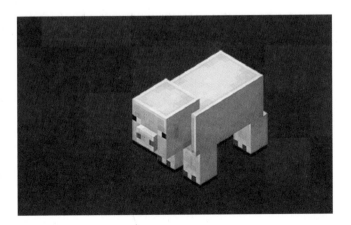

PAPER

Paper is a crafting resource only item—you use it only for making other things, like books. You can craft paper from sugarcane, and you can find it in some Adventure chests.

PARROT

Parrots are rare denizens of the jungle and are known to mimic the sounds of nearby hostile mobs. If you kill them, they will only drop a few feathers, at most. You can find them in jungle buildplates, in some Adventure chests, and some Adventures. [Health: 6]

PEONY

The Peony is a two-block tall pink flower that you can craft into pink dye. You can find peonies in a few buildplates.

PICKAXE

A pickaxe (often called just a "pick") is a tool you use to mine (or break) stone and ore blocks. The better the material used to craft the pick, the faster it will break blocks and the more durable it is (the longer it will last). Also—the better the material used to craft the pick, the more kinds of blocks a pick can mine.

- **Wood/Gold picks:** Stone and stone variants and coal ore.
- **Stone picks:** Same as wood picks, as well as iron ore.
- **Iron picks:** Same as stone picks, and gold ore, redstone, and diamond.
- **Diamond picks:** Same as iron picks, plus obsidian blocks.

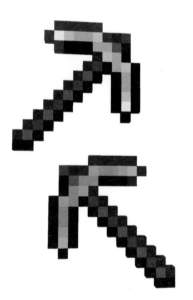

PIEBALD PIG

"Piebald" means colored with patches of two colors, usually black and white. The Minecraft Earth Piebald pig has brown splotches on a cream coat. [Health: 10]

PIG

The pig is a Minecraft classic, and classic Minecraft even has hostile Nether mobs based on it and allows players to ride on pig. Minecraft Earth has included the beloved pig along with a host of variants for collecting and farming, including Muddy pigs, Pale pigs, Piebald pigs, and Spotted pigs. Pigs drop raw pork when they are killed, and you can find pigs in Pig tappables, buildplates, and Adventures. [Health: 10]

PIG TAPPABLE

Pig tappables are one of the four mob tappables, and will give you a pig or possibly one of the rarer variants: the Spotted pig, the Muddy pig, the Pale pig, or Piebald pig.

PLANKS

Planks are wood blocks created by crafting wooden logs by themselves in the Crafting interface. Different logs will give differently textured wood plank. Wood planks are the resource for many Minecraft recipes, from wooden tools, to sticks, to bowls. Most recipes that require planks don't care what type of wood you use. For some recipes like doors and fences, the crafted result will be the color of the planks you used. For example, to craft a jungle fence, you'll need jungle wood. You can find oak planks in Chest tappables, and all types of planks in various Adventures and buildplates.

PLAY MODE

The button to the right of the Build button will get you into Play mode.

In Play mode, you can place your buildplate at "real life" size and, through your mobile's screen, walk around it. Any changes you make in this mode aren't saved. Your buildplate will remain the same as it was before you entered Play Mode. In Play mode, you can choose either Punch Mode or Interact mode to interact with the scene.

POLAR BEAR

The Polar bear is a neutral mob that inhabits Minecraft's snowy and frozen biomes. It will become hostile if attacked or you get too close to its cub (or attack it). If you kill them, they'll drop raw cod or salmon. You can find them in some Adventures and buildplates. [Health: 30]

POND TAPPABLE

The Pond tappable looks very similar to the Grass tappable but has a block of water at its top. It gives many of the same resources as Grass tappables as well as some resources somewhat associated with water or ponds, including clay, glow squid, salmon, squid, sugarcane, and tropical slime.

POPPIES

Poppies are a small red flower found in many Minecraft biomes that you can use to make red dye. You can get them from Grass and Pond tappables, Adventures, and buildplates.

POTATO

The potato is a food and crop that you can grow on farmland to make more potatoes. You plant the whole potato to grow the plant, and it will grow through several stages. When its leaves are full and tall and you can see the tops of potatoes, you can harvest the plant for up to five more potatoes. By itself, a raw potato isn't very health-restoring, but you can bake potatoes for a good food source. You can get potatoes as loot from common Adventure chests.

POWERED RAILS

Powered rails are a type of rail placed next to each other to make tracks for minecarts to travel on. Powered rails are used to make minecarts begin moving from a resting position as well as continue moving along a track. They are also necessary to stop minecarts sliding backwards on a lengthy climbing track. In general, place a powered rail for every 10 regular rails horizontally, and at least three powered rails for every six rails on an upward slope. Use power from a lever or a redstone block to keep powered rails powered. One powered power rail will itself power up to eight rails in one direction. You can find powered rails in Chest tappables, Adventure chests, and some Adventures.

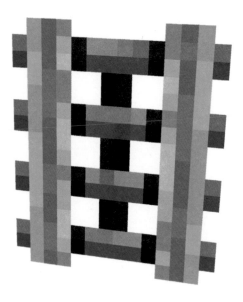

PRESSURE PLATES

Pressure plates are redstone components that deliver a redstone signal to an adjacent block when entities (mobs, players, fallen or dropped items) are on top of it. There are several types of pressure plates:

- **Wood pressure plate:** Detects any entities; always delivers full strength redstone signal (15).

- **Stone pressure plate:** Only detects mobs; always delivers full strength redstone signal (15).

- **Iron weighted pressure plate:** Detects any entities; delivers strength from 1 to 15 relative to the number of entities on it, from 1 to 141 and over.

- **Gold weighted pressure plate:** Detects any entities: delivers strength from 1 to 15 relative to the number of entities from 1 to 15 and over.

PROFILE

Your profile icon, at the top left of the World Map, shows your current status in the game.

The number at the bottom is your current experience level and the yellow border shows your progress towards the next level. To the right is your health bar. Click on your profile icon to open the Profile page, which has more details about your profile, and links to the Character creator, Activity Log, and Settings. At the bottom of the Profile page are more details about your experience level, and gold icons. Click a gold icon to see what stat it represents and what your statistic is for that, from Mobs Collected to Tools Broken.

PUMPKIN

Pumpkins are another food crop you can grow on watered farmland from pumpkin seeds. They grow like melons—first a stalk grows, then a full pumpkin block will appear next to and attached to the stalk. To harvest, break just the pumpkin and leave the stalk to grow another one.

PUMPKIN PIE

Take a pumpkin, sugar from a sugarcane, and an egg and you can craft a partially eaten pumpkin pie. If you eat the pie, you'll get 4 health points (HP) restored.

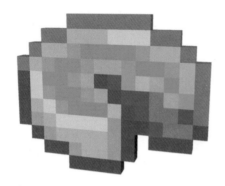

PUMPKIN SEEDS

You'll need these to grow pumpkins, and you can find them in Grass and Pond tappables and sometimes in Adventure chests.

PUNCH MODE

In Punch mode, you can "punch" or repeatedly click blocks without a tool to break soft blocks like sand and wood, but you will still need the right tool for harder blocks.

PUZZLE ADVENTURES

Some Adventures have puzzles to solve in order to finish the Adventure and get the Adventure chest. These puzzles may be things like broken rails you need to repair, empty flowerpots that need to be filled, or a sequence of lamps that is missing a lamp or two. A good indication that you are playing a puzzle Adventure is the presence of just a few unusual blocks or a set of blocks that looks broken or is missing something.

QUARTZ

Quartz is a popular building block in Minecraft that is crafted from four Nether quartz. You can craft it into quartz slabs and stairs, as well as pillar quartz blocks. You can craft two quartz slabs into the chiseled quartz block. You can smelt quartz blocks into smooth quartz blocks that can themselves be used to create smooth quartz slabs and stairs.

Clockwise from top left: Quartz, chiseled quartz, pillar quartz, and smooth quartz.

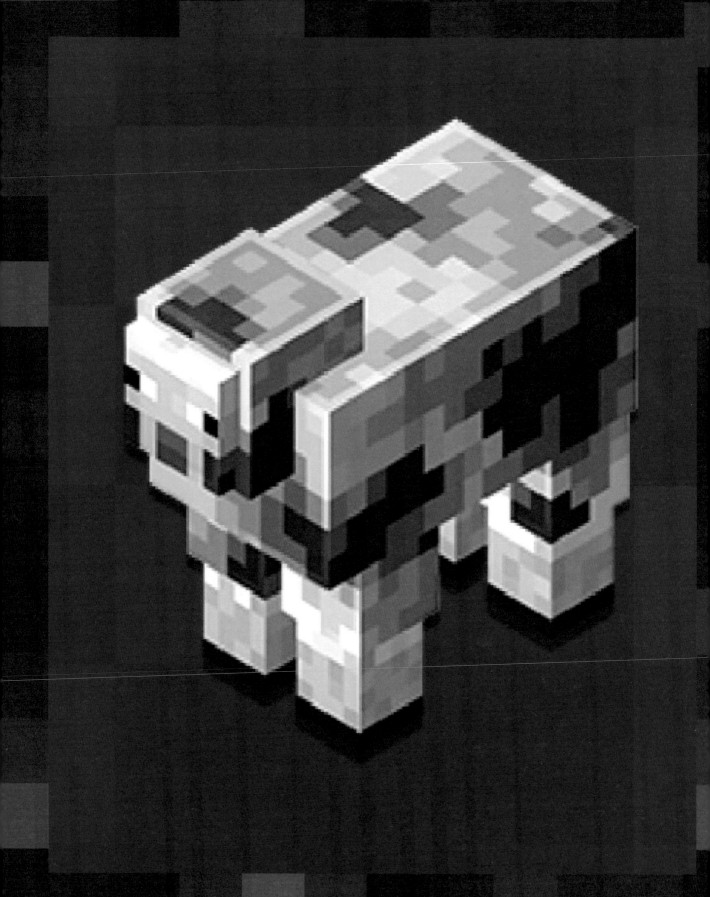

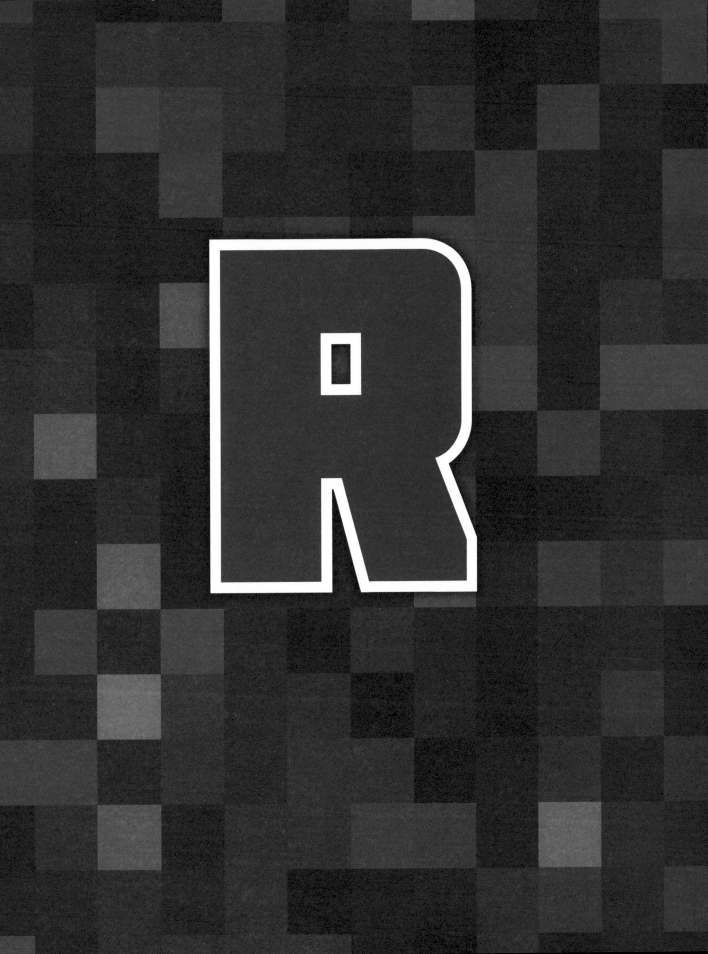

RABBIT

The Minecraft Earth rabbit is a sandy-furred, desert-loving creature, and the easiest way to find it is to download one of the desert-themed buildplates. When they are killed, rabbits drop raw rabbit, rabbit hide, and more rarely a rabbit foot. You can find them in some Adventures and buildplates. [Health: 3]

RABBIT STEW

Rabbit stew is one of the best, or most replenishing, foods in Minecraft, as well as one

of the more difficult to craft. You'll need cooked rabbit, a carrot, a baked potato, a mushroom (either kind) and a bowl. Eating it will restore 8 health points.

RADIUS BOOST

The radius boost increases your avatar's radius (also called the Player interaction radius) on the World Map. Level I adds 35m for 10 minutes; Level II adds 53m for 15 minutes; and Level III adds 70m for 30 minutes. You can also get a radius boost of 35m for 10 minutes from the Minecraft Earth mini-figures "Seeking Dolphin" and "Seeking Wolf."

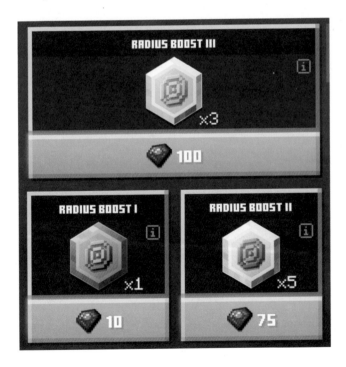

RAILS

Rails are Minecraft blocks that make a path for moving minecarts on, and you place them next to each other on blocks to create tracks. Rails can be placed diagonally on blocks that rise up (or down) one block height at a time. They will also curve when you place them at right angles. You need to use powered rails along with rails to keep minecarts going. There are also several types of specialty rails: activator rails and detector rails.

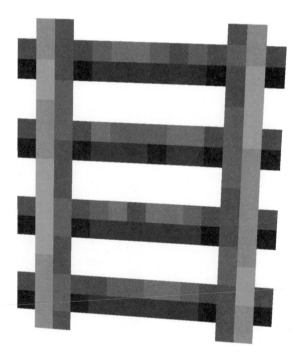

RARITY

Blocks, items, mobs, Adventures, Adventure chests, and many challenges are given a rarity level that corresponds either to how rare that resource is or how difficult/high-level. There are five levels: common, uncommon, rare, epic, and legendary. Tappables include more common, uncommon, and rare resources, while the most legendary items are found in high-level Adventures or by crafting them. Each rarity level has a color associated with it. You'll see this color around items in your inventory and as borders around tappables you are opening.

- Common: Gray
- Uncommon: Green
- Rare: Blue
- Epic: Purple
- Legendary: Gold

REDSTONE

Redstone dust, also called redstone,[1] is a power transmitting block that looks like a little glittery piece of dust when you place it on a block. You place redstone dust on adjacent blocks to make lines of redstone that can transmit redstone power between a power source and a redstone mechanism. When redstone dust is powered, it

---

1   The word *redstone* can also refer to the overall redstone power system used to make contraptions in Minecraft. For instance, "I am going to do a little redstone today," means you are going to play around with redstone contraptions.

lights up. A line of redstone dust can only carry a power signal 15 blocks, and with each block, the power signal decreases by 1. (You can reset the power to 15 by inserting a repeater into the line of redstone.)

You can mine redstone ore in Adventures which will drop redstone, and you can find redstone dust in Stone tappables.

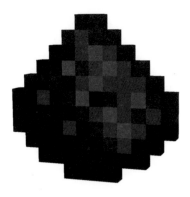

REDSTONE BLOCK

Redstone blocks are a redstone power source that emits a constant, full-strength power signal of 15 on all sides. You can find redstone blocks in some Adventures or Adventure chests and you craft blocks of redstone from 9 redstone dust.

REDSTONE COMPARATORS

Redstone comparators are a redstone component that will take a redstone signal coming in from the back and others coming in from the sides and emit a signal from the front. It has two modes: Compare and Subtract. Compare mode is the default state, with the front torch unlit. If you right-click the comparator, it enters Subtract mode and the front torch lights up.

In Compare mode, it emits no signal if any side signal is greater than the back signal. If the rear signal is stronger than both of the side signals (or if there are no side signals), it transmits a signal with the strength of the rear signal.

In subtract mode, the comparator subtracts the strength of the highest side signal from the rear signal and emits a signal with the new calculated strength.

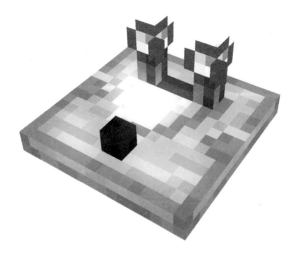

REDSTONE COMPONENTS

Redstone components are Minecraft blocks that are used to manage or transmit power or react to redstone power in some way. They include:

- Redstone repeaters
- Note blocks
- Powered rails
- Redstone lamps
- Tripwire hooks
- Doors, trapdoors, and gates

REDSTONE LAMP

Redstone lamps will light up if you power them with a redstone signal. You craft them from redstone dust and glowstone, and you can also find them in Chest tappables and some Adventures, Adventure chests, and buildplates.

REDSTONE ORE

Redstone ore is an ore you can find in Minecraft that will drop redstone dust when you mine it, and you will need an iron or diamond pick to do so. You'll find it in many Adventures.

REDSTONE POWER

Redstone power is a little like electricity and is used to power things, like opening doors and moving minecarts. Minecraft has special functional blocks, or redstone components, that emit or transmit power and or react in some way when power is sent to them. Redstone power sources include:

- Redstone torch
- Redstone block
- Button
- Activator rail

- Lever
- Pressure plate

Once created, redstone power can travel through a line of redstone dust for up to 15 blocks. A full strength power signal coming from a power source is 15, and power decreases in strength each block it travels through redstone dust.

REDSTONE REPEATER

A redstone repeater is a redstone component that transmits redstone power coming in from the rear through its front. It also resets a fading signal to full-strength, or 15. That means if you want to carry a redstone signal for more than 15 blocks, you would use a repeater in the line of redstone.

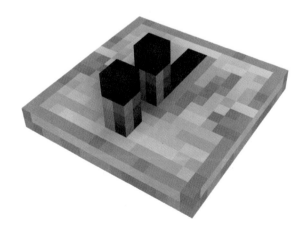

REDSTONE TORCH

A redstone torch is a redstone power source, and emits a constant, full-strength power signal of 15. It sends power to adjacent redstone dust, comparators, repeaters, and other components, and to a solid block above it. It doesn't give power to the block it is placed on. Also, if you send power to a redstone torch, it will turn off and emit no power.

ROCKY SHEEP

This Minecraft Earth variant of the classic sheep mob has a white and brownish pattern that kind of resembles rocks. You can find it in Sheep tappables.

ROSE BUSH

The rose bush is a two-tall flower that you can craft into red dye. You can find them in Grass and Pond tappables as well as some Adventures and the Dark and Shroomy buildplate.

ROTTEN FLESH

Rotten flesh is dropped by zombies when you kill them, and it is not quite clear if it is the Zombie's own flesh or if it is the snack they were munching on. In Minecraft, you can eat it if you are desperate although it may poison you.

RUBIES

Rubies are the in-game currency. You can purchase them directly through the Shop (40 rubies cost $1.99) or you can earn them through gameplay. Rubies are randomly awarded to you when you collect tappables. Completing challenges can also gift you rubies.

Rubies are one of the in-game currencies used for microtransactions; you can purchase them in multiples in the Store.

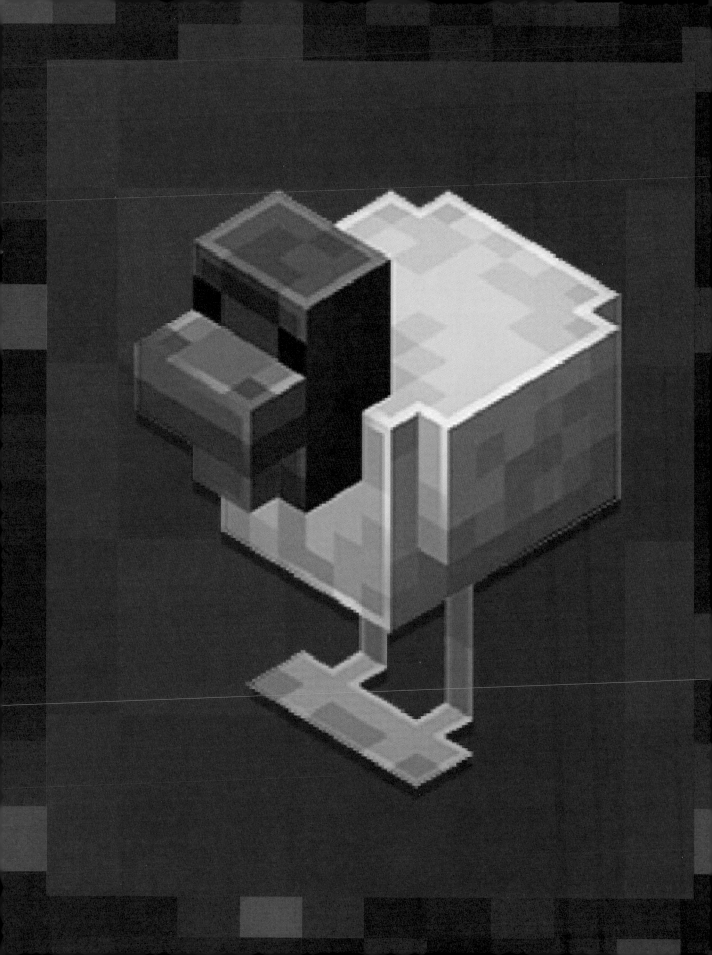

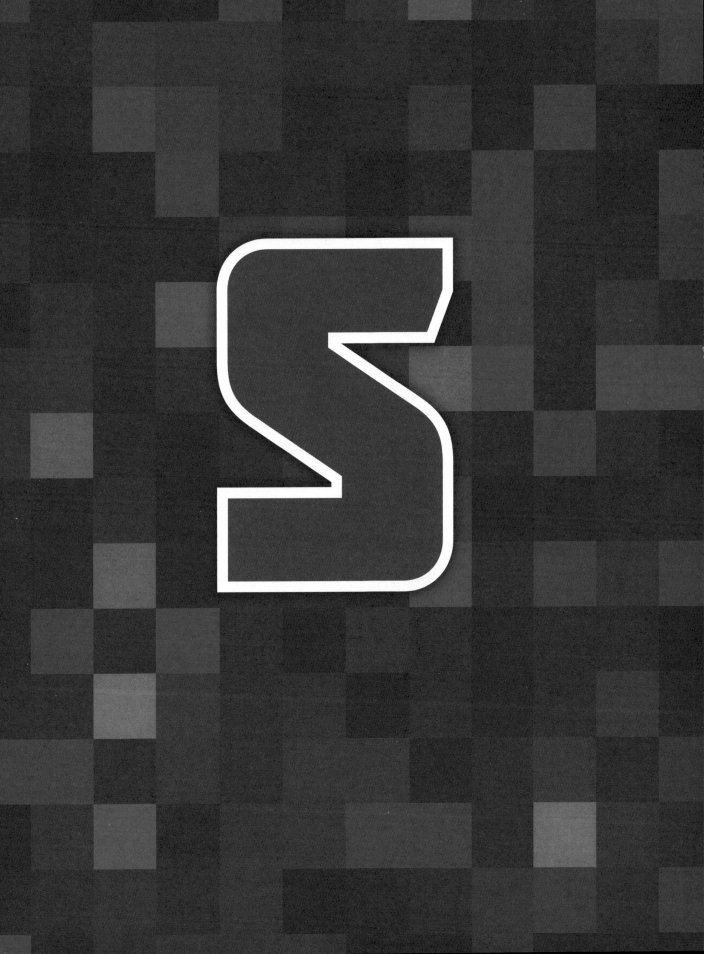

SALMON

Salmon are a colorful red fish that you can kill and cook into an excellent food. You could also place them in a peaceful, safe pool on a buildplate. Killing them will give you raw salmon and occasionally bones. You can find them in Pond tappables. [Health: 3]

SAND

Sand is one of the few blocks in Minecraft that are affected by gravity; that is, it will fall if the block beneath it is removed. If the falling sand lands on a solid block, like stone, the sand will stay in its block form. If the falling sand lands on a non-solid block like a torch, it will revert

into its item shape. An orange-red variant of sand is called Red Sand. You can find sand in Stone tappables as well as Adventures and buildplates.

SANDSTONE

Sandstone is a block that looks like a hardened, compressed sand and is often found in desert biomes below several layers of sand blocks.

From left to right, sandstone, chiseled sandstone, cut sandstone, and smooth sandstone. Below are the same varieties in red sandstone.

It is a popular building material. A reddish-orange variant is Red Sandstone. You can craft sandstone into slabs and stairs, as well as cut sandstone. You can craft sandstone slabs into chiseled sandstone, and smelt sandstone into smooth sandstone. You can craft sandstone blocks themselves from 4 sand and you can find sandstone in Adventures and buildplates.

SAPLINGS

Saplings are items you plant to grow trees and they look like mini versions of the tree. You can plant them on dirt and dirt variants like grass and coarse dirt, and you can make them grow faster by using bone meal on them. You can place them in flowerpots for decoration and use them as a fuel source. Saplings need space, about 2 blocks on all sides and more above, in order to grow, although you can grow some saplings right next to each other. If you're having trouble growing a sapling, give it more space.

SEAGRASS

Seagrass is an underwater plant that you can grow by using bone meal on most blocks that are under two blocks of water. You can harvest it only with shears.

SEASONAL CHALLENGES

Seasonal Challenges are a set of themed, temporary challenges that usually last about two weeks. Past themes have been Nature, Dark Forest, and Grassy Plains. Each season has a tree of challenges that unlock as you progress. Completing each challenge in the tree will grant you some goodies, and you'll get even more if you finish the entire tree. Click the Globe icon in the sidebar to access these challenges.

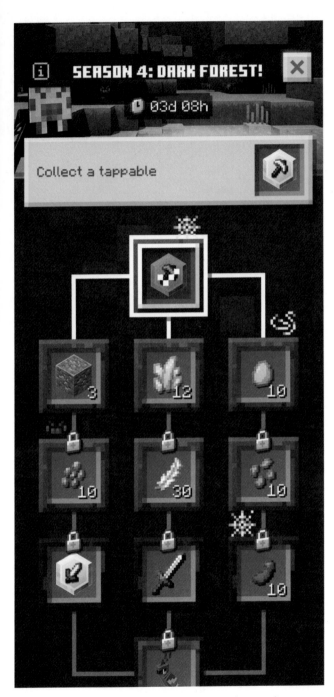

The icons in the Seasonal Challenges show what your rewards are for completing each task. They can be anything from simple items to boosts, weapons, and rare mobs.

SHEARS

Shears are a tool you use to clip wool blocks from sheep. You can also use shears on a few blocks to get that block rather than its common drop: A cobweb, which usually drops string; leaf blocks, which usually are just destroyed or may drop an apple; and vines, which are otherwise just destroyed. You craft shears from two iron ingots.

SHEEP

The classic Minecraft sheep can be shorn with shears for its wool. It will need to eat a bit of grass in order to grow more wool, so if you are planning to keep a herd of sheep, make sure there are enough grass blocks for them to eat and to regenerate missing grass. You can also dye white sheep one of 15 other colors by using a piece of dye on them. If you kill a sheep, it may drop raw mutton and wool. There are a number of sheep variants, including Flecked Sheep, Inky Sheep, Rocky Sheep, and the Horned Sheep. You can find sheep in Sheep tappables and in some Adventures and buildplates. [Health: 8]

variants, like rocky sheep, flecked sheep, inky sheep, or horned sheep.

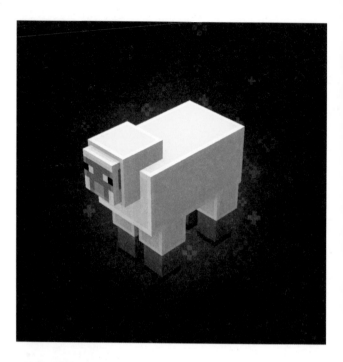

SHOVEL

A shovel is a tool you use to break "softer" block: dirt, gravel, and sand. They are made from a single tool material block (wood planks,

SHEEP TAPPABLE

Sheep tappables are one of the four Mob tappables on the World screen. Tapping them will usually get you a regular white sheep, but you have a chance to get one of the other

cobblestone, gold, iron ingot, diamond.) and the better the material, the longer the shovel will last and the faster it will break blocks. You can get shovels sometimes from Adventure chests.

SKELETON

Minecraft's skeletons come with a bone-jangling clatter and a deadly accurate bow. They never run out of arrows, and once they spot you they will follow you and attack you until one of you wins. When you kill them, they may drop arrows and/or bones. You can find them in Adventures and very rarely in Stone tappables.

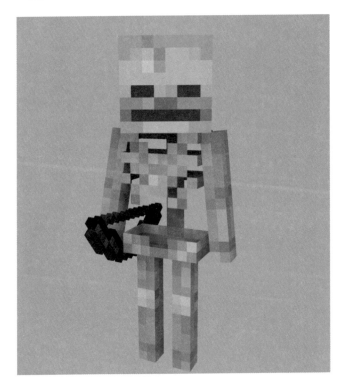

SKELETON WOLF

Minecraft Earth has hybridized skeletons and hostile wolves to make this dangerous skeleton wolf with a bone-shattering howl. You can find them rarely in Stone tappables and also in some Adventures, and they'll drop bones when you kill them.

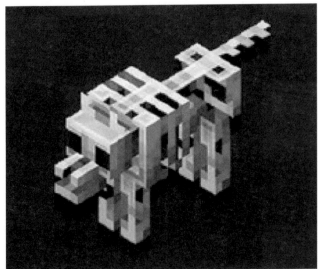

SLABS

Slabs are blocks that take up half the space of a block. They're often mistakenly referred to as "half slabs"—which would make them quarter blocks! They can be placed in the top half of a block's cubic area or the bottom half, and sometimes are called top slabs and bottom slabs when their position needs to be specified. Many (but not all) of Minecraft's building blocks come with slab variants, including wood planks, stones, sandstones, and bricks.

SMELTING

Minecraft smelting is the process of cooking resources in a furnace to create new resources.

You can use the furnace to cook raw meats, turn clay into bricks, and smelt iron and gold ores into ingots. There are some decorative blocks that you can only get through smelting, like glass blocks and terracotta. You can find the Smelting interface by clicking the Make Stuff icon on the bottom menu bar. Here you can scroll through, filter, and sort recipes for smelting. Recipes that you don't have the resources for are grayed out.

SMELTING BOOST

Smelting takes time, and if you have the rubies to pay for it, you can use a Smelting Boost to make it faster. Level I grants you increased speed of 10% for 10 minutes, Level II increases the speed by 20% for 15 minutes, and Level

III ups the speed by 30% for 30 minutes. The mini-figure "Smelting Blaze" will also improve your smelting speeds by 10% for 10 minutes.

SNOW

Snow blocks are terrain blocks in Minecraft that you find in frozen and snowy biomes. Snow layers are thinner blocks, 1/8 of a full block height, that may also cover the ground in these biomes. Snow layers are also deposited by melon golems as they wander about, and multiple layers can be placed on top of one another. Breaking snow blocks and snow layers with a shovel will drop snow balls. You can craft snow blocks into snow layers and vice versa. You will find snow blocks and snow layers in some Adventures and buildplates.

SNOWBALL

Snowballs are Minecraft projectiles—you can actually throw them, though they won't cause any damage to mobs. You can get snowballs by breaking snow blocks or layers with a shovel. You can also craft four snowballs into a block of snow.

SPIDER

Minecraft's spiders unfortunately are the giant kind, close to the size of a player, and they are not your friend. They can scale up vertical

walls to jump on you and attack you. Try to get them before they bounce up at you! They'll drop string when you kill them, and you can find them in Adventure chests, Adventures, the Sand Sanctuary buildplate, and very rarely in Oak tappables.

SPOTTED PIG

The Spotted Pig is a light pink pig that has dark brownish-black spots, and you can find it in Pig tappables. [Health: 10]

SPRUCE LEAVES

Spruce leaves are used as the canopy for spruce trees. They have a distinctive, small-leafed and grayish green pattern; and their color doesn't change in different biomes. Shear them to get the entire block; break them or let them decay for a chance of a stick or sapling.

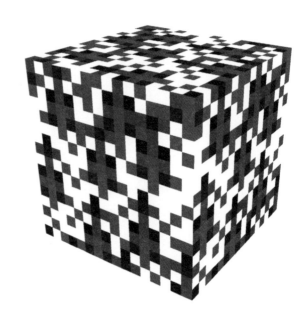

SPRUCE LOGS

Spruce log blocks are used for the trunks of spruce trees. You can use them as decorative blocks or fuel, craft them into planks, or use an axe to strip their bark. You can find these logs in Spruce tappables and in some Adventures and buildplates.

SPRUCE SAPLINGS

To grow a spruce tree, you'll need a spruce sapling; to grow a giant spruce tree, you'll need four planted in a square. You can find spruce saplings in Spruce tappables and as drops from Spruce leaf blocks.

SPRUCE TAPPABLE

The Spruce tappable is one of the three tree tappables in Minecraft Earth, and tapping it will get you spruce logs and sapling. The spruce sapling is an epic rarity, so if you're given a challenge to get an Epic tappable, a spruce tappable is a good bet.

SPRUCE TREE

The spruce tree is one of Minecraft's six tree types, and it is found in taiga, mountain, and snowy biomes. You grow it from a spruce sapling—and you can also grow a giant spruce

tree from placing four saplings in a square. As with any tree, you can break its blocks with your hand or an axe and you will get spruce logs. You can craft the logs into planks which you can then use in recipes requiring wood, as a fuel, or as a building block. You can find spruce saplings in Spruce tappables, and spruce trees and logs in some Adventures and buildplates.

SPRUCE WOOD PLANKS

Spruce wood planks are crafted from spruce logs and can be used in recipes requiring wood planks. You can also use these planks to create spruce buttons, pressure plates, fences, gates, doors, slabs, and stairs.

SQUID

The gentle squid is a Minecraft mob you will find bobbing about in rivers and oceans. It will open and close its tentacles as it swims about, revealing a large mouth at the bottom of its body. They need water to survive, so on a buildplate they should be placed in a pond. If you kill them, they'll drop ink sacs. You can find squid in Pond tappables.

STACKS

In your main inventory, items of the same type are stored in one slot—you can have 1000 oak logs, and they will just take up one square. That slot filled with items is called a stack of that item. Your hotbar works differently: The biggest size for a stack is 64, and only one tool, weapon, or bucket can be stored in a slot at a time.

STAIRS

Stairs are blocks that let you move up and down without having to jump. They're crafted from six blocks of some building materials, like wood planks, sandstone, quartz, stone and stone variants, bricks, and cobblestone. They're often used decoratively to make roofs and patterned walls and other structures. You can find some stair blocks in Chest tappables, as well as many Adventures and buildplates.

STICK

Sticks are a useful resource in Minecraft and are used in many crafting recipes, notably for all handheld weapons and tools as well as fences. You craft four sticks from two wood planks, and sticks are sometimes a drop from decaying leaf blocks.

STONE

Stone is one of the most common blocks in Minecraft and is found in abundance below ground level, along with patches of earth, gravel, and other stone types. When you mine it, it will drop cobblestone. You can smelt cobblestone to turn it back into stone. You can craft it into stone slabs and stairs as well as stone bricks, and stone blocks are also used in many crafting recipes. You can find stone blocks in Chest tappables, Adventures, and buildplates.

STONE BRICKS

Stone bricks are a very popular building block and you can craft them from four stone. You can craft stone bricks into slabs and stair blocks and stone brick walls. Stone brick slabs can be crafted into chiseled stone blocks, and you can smelt stone bricks into cracked stone bricks, a great block for making buildings looked ruined. You can find stone brick blocks in Chest tappables, as well as Adventures and buildplates.

diorite, flint, granite, redstone, sand, stone, and very rarely a skeleton, furnace golem, or skeleton wolf.

STONE TAPPABLE

Stone tappables are one of the three environmental tappables that give you natural resources related to the terrain. Stone tappables may contain 1 to 3 of the following resources: andesite, brown mushrooms, cobblestone,

STORE

The Store is an area in the game where you can purchase some buildplates and boosts, and the rubies you'll need to use as currency. You can also earn rubies through gameplay to use at the store.

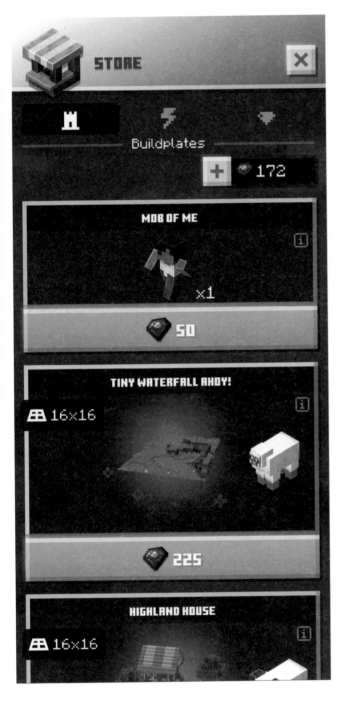

STORMY CHICKEN

This somewhat rare chicken variant has a dark gray head, gray feathers, and a deep amber beak. Like a regular chicken, it may drop a few feathers and raw chicken if you kill it. You can find the Stormy chicken in Chicken tappables.

STRING

String is a crafting resource that you can get from breaking cobwebs or killing spiders. For example, it can be used to make white wool and bows and is used in tripwire traps. You can find string in common Adventure chests and in some Adventures.

STRIPPED LOGS

You can right-click any wood log with an axe to create a Stripped log—the log without the heavy texture of its bark surfaces—and this is useful as a decoration block.

SUGAR CANE

Sugar Cane is a plant that grows 3 blocks high and you can harvest it to make sugar and paper. To grow it, you must place a sugarcane block on grass or sand and next to a block of water. To avoid replanting, harvest just the top two blocks of sugarcane.

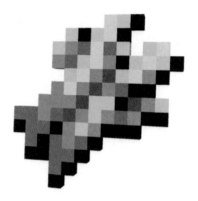

SUGAR

Sugar is a crafting resource that you create from sugarcane and use in recipes like pumpkin pie.

SUNFLOWERS

Sunflowers are a two-tall flower that you can use to create yellow dye. You can find them in Grass and Pond tappables and some Adventures.

SUNSET COW

The sunset cow is a bright orange and black variant of the classic Minecraft cow. You can find it in Cow tappables and in some Adventures. [Health: 10]

SWORD

The sword is your primary weapon in Minecraft Earth. It acts as a ranged weapon, so you can attack mobs at a distance with it. Swords are crafted with one stick and two items of the material you choose. You can choose from (in order of damage the sword can do): wood, gold ingots, stone, iron ingots, or diamonds. To use a sword, select it in your hotbar, move your crossbar or cursor over the mob, and click away.

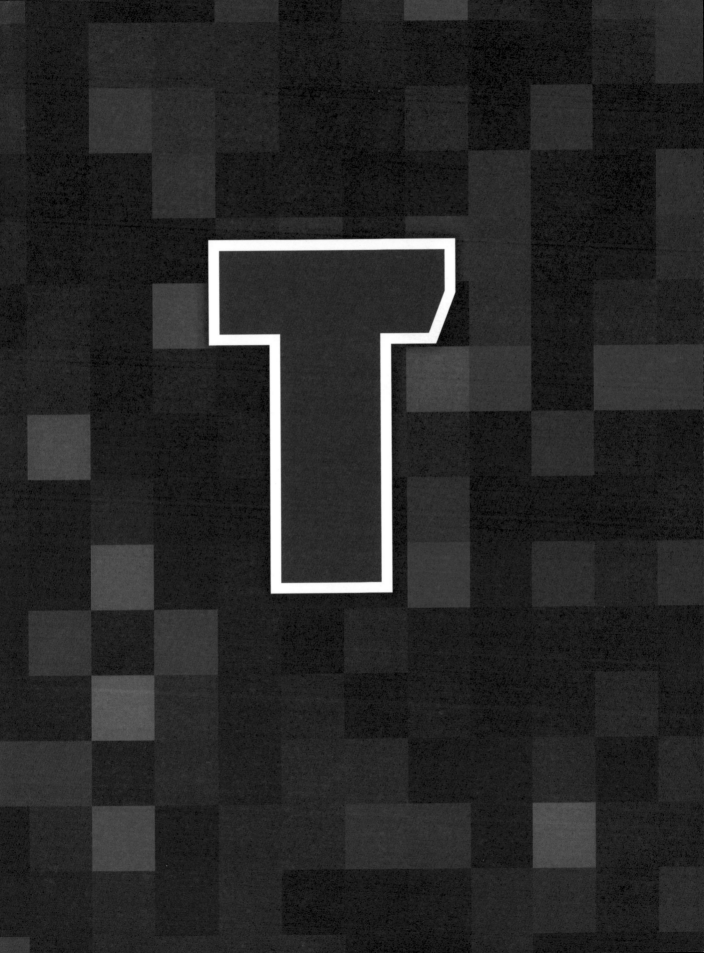

TAPPABLES

Tappables are a primary way of collecting resources, plants, and animals in Minecraft Earth. You'll need to move so that your avatar's radius in the World Map covers the tappable, and then you can click on its icon to open it and get its contents. The goods will automatically be delivered to your inventory. There are Stone tappables, Grass tappables, Pond tappables, Oak tappables, Spruce tappables, Birch tappables, and Chest tappables. The different tappables have different types of resources; for example, Grass tappables have plant and earthy resources.

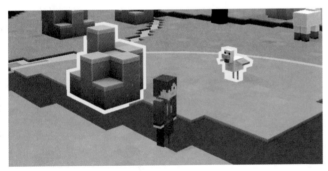

Tappables are found on your main screen, the World Map. You can only open tappables that are in your player radius—like this Chicken and Pond tappable here.

TAPPABLE CHALLENGES

As you walk around collecting tappables, you'll occasionally get challenges under the "Tappable" category. You'll notice these being given to you when an icon of a piece of paper pops up on the World Map screen and jumps into the Challenges trophy icon. There are four levels of tappable challenges; common, uncommon, rare, and epic; the higher levels are harder but offer more experience points (XP). If you don't want to do a particular challenge, you can click the trash icon next to the challenge's title.

Tappable challenges are challenges you get from collecting tappables.

TERRACOTTA

Terracotta is a decorative building block in Minecraft that is created by smelting clay blocks. You can dye terracotta into sixteen additional colors using dyes. You can also smelt the dyed terracotta to get brightly patterned glazed terracotta blocks. You can get terracotta from some Adventure chests and occasionally in some Adventures.

At the top is the terracotta block, made of smelting clay, and below it are the 16 colored terracotta blocks that you craft from combining brownish terracotta with Minecraft's 16 colored dyes.

TOOLS

Minecraft Earth tools include axes, flint and steel, hoes, shears, and shovels. Tools, like weapons, can be made out of different materials, and the material determines how fast the tool works and how long it lasts. In increasing effectiveness, tool materials are gold, wood, stone, iron, and diamond. Gold is an expensive material that isn't very durable and is usually a poor choice for a tool or weapon. An iron pickaxe or better is needed to mine gold ore and diamonds.

TORCH

A torch is a source of light in Minecraft. You can craft four from one stick and one coal (or charcoal) and when you place it down in a dark area, it will light that area up. This can be handy in the dark recesses of some Adventure dungeons.

TRAPDOOR

Trapdoors are 1x1 doors (and redstone components) that can be placed vertically or horizontally. Mobs that can fit in the 1x1 opening can move through them. If they're made from wood, they can be opened with a right-click or a redstone pulse; iron trapdoors can only open with a redstone signal. Trapdoors are often used as barriers to prevent players and mobs from falling down a hole, or decoratively, as window shutters for example.

TRIPWIRE HOOK

Tripwire hooks are used in duos to set up tripwire traps. You place them opposite each other, on the sides of blocks, up to 40 blocks apart. You then right-click 1 string on one of the hooks to create the tripwire. Now, when an entity crosses through that string, the tripwire hooks emit a redstone pulse. What you do then is up to you!

TROPICAL FISH

This orange and white striped tropical fish resembles a real world clownfish. If you kill it, it will drop raw fish, and more rarely, bones. However, you can't cook the fish or eat it. You can find tropical fish when you use a bucket on a Tropical Slime. When you do this, you'll have a bucket of tropical fish, which you can use to keep the fish or place them in water.

TROPICAL SLIME

The Minecraft Earth neutral cousin of Minecraft's hostile green swampy Slimes, the Tropical slime is a large hopping cube of blue slime that hosts an interior duo of tropical fish. You can kill the slime and recover the tropical fish by using a bucket on it. You can find it rarely in Pond tappables and some Adventures.

[Health: 16]

TULIPS

There are four differently colored tulip flowers in Minecraft: orange, pink, red, and white. You can use them to craft dyes, and you can find them in Grass and Pond tappables and in some buildplates.

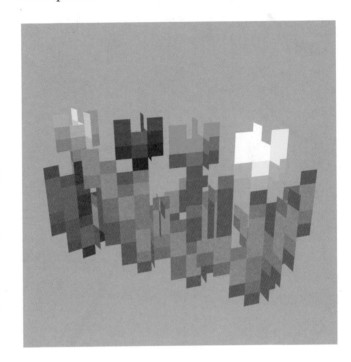

U-V-W
X-Y-Z

VESTED RABBIT

The vested rabbit is colored white and gray and it is a very rare find in Grass and Pond tappables. If you kill it, it can drop raw rabbit, rabbit hide, and rarely a rabbit's foot. [Health: 3]

VINES

Vines are a plant block that can be placed only on other blocks. They can grow upwards and to the side, as long as there is a block to attach to, and downwards even if there are no blocks to attach to. They can't be grown with bone meal, but you can craft them with cobblestone and stone bricks to make mossy cobblestone and mossy stone bricks. Vines are generated on jungle trees and terrain. To gather them as a resource, use shears. You can find them in Adventure chests and in some buildplates.

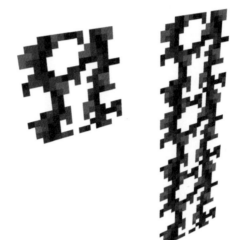

WALLS

Walls are a block that act as a barrier to mobs and are also used as a decorative block. They join or attach to each other when you place them

in adjacent blocks. You can craft them from different stone and brick materials, including stone brick, mossy stone brick, cobblestone, mossy cobblestone, and sandstone. You can find them in some Adventures and buildplates.

WATER

Water is a block in Minecraft, even though it doesn't look or always seem to behave like one. A water source block will spread up to 7 blocks away, and it and the flowing water blocks will uproot many types of items, like plants, rails, flowerpots, redstone dust, and some redstone components. When you pick up a water source block with a bucket, it will remove the water source and its flow, and the bucket will become a bucket of water. You can then place the water down again with the bucket. It is possible to create an "infinite source" of water, by placing two water source blocks one block away from each other. The two source blocks placed in this way will always combine to make the central block a water source block. Another way to create an infinite source of water is to fill just two corners of a 2x2 hole with water source blocks. These two water blocks combine to make their two neighboring, diagonal blocks (the other corners) also water. This feature means that if you want to fill a square pool with water, you

only have to place a water source block every other block along two adjacent sides the pool, and these water source blocks will combine to fill up the whole pool.

Here are two types of infinite water pools. One is three blocks long, and there are two source blocks at either end that must remain in order to keep the central infinite water block. The square pool has four water source blocks and you can pick up water from any corner.

WEAPONS

The primary weapons in Minecraft Earth are swords and bows. They are both ranged weapons, meaning you can strike mobs from afar. You can often use other items in battle: flint and steel will set things alight, including TNT, and you can pour buckets of lava to damage mobs below you. As with tools, weapons can be made out of different materials, and the material determines how fast the tool works and how long it lasts. In increasing effectiveness, tool materials are wood, stone, gold, iron, and diamond. Gold isn't very durable and is usually a poor choice for a tool or weapon.

WHEAT

Wheat is a crop plant you can grow on watered farmland by planting wheat seeds. Wheat has several growing stages, and in the final stage it loses any tinges of green. You can craft bread from wheat, as well as cookies (with cocoa beans), and hay bales (which you can also craft back into wheat).

WHEAT SEEDS

You'll need these seeds to grow wheat to make bread and other foods; they are sometimes dropped when you break grass. Otherwise, you can get them from common Adventure chests and Grass and Pond tappables.

WOOL

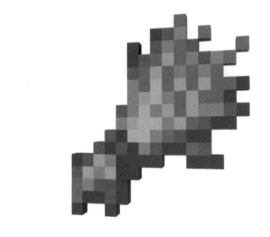

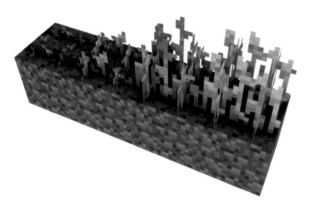

Blocks of wool can be shorn from sheep (or dropped by sheep when they are killed) and used in crafting recipes or as decorative blocks. You can dye wool blocks with dyes, and craft it into colored carpet as well. You can find wool in some Adventures, and you can craft white wool from 4 string.

WOOLY COW

Wool isn't just from sheep anymore! This fuzzy cousin of the Minecraft cow is an inhabitant of the Ice Plains biome, and you can use shears on it to get some nice brown wool. You can get it from Cow tappables, in some Adventures, and in the Highland Grazing buildplate. Like a regular cow, it will drop raw beef and leather if you kill it. [Health: 10]

WORLD MAP

The World Map is your main and opening screen in Minecraft Earth. It displays a map of streets at your current location, dotted with tappables that you can collect. The map updates as you walk around. The World Map screen also displays your Profile icon, the compass, a sidebar menu linking to your Journal, Seasonal Challenges, Challenges, and Boosts. On the bottom menu are links to your inventory, the Make Stuff area (Crafting and Smelting), Adventures, buildplates, and the Store. You can change the size of the World Map by pinching or spreading the map image and rotate it by dragging in a circle.

ZOMBIE

Zombies are a classic, original Minecraft hostile, and they are just as hostile in Minecraft Earth. They will attack you if they can find a way to climb out of the dungeons and get to you. (Or if they spawn right on the ground in a high-level Adventure!). When you kill them, they drop zombie flesh, and more rarely iron ingots and carrots. You can find them in Adventure chests, Adventures, and in the Secluded Mine buildplate.